Academic Library Makerspaces

Academic Library Makerspaces

A Practical Guide to Planning, Collaborating, and Supporting Campus Innovation

Katy B. Mathuews and Daniel J. Harper

LIBRARIES UNLIMITED®
An Imprint of ABC-CLIO, LLC
Santa Barbara, California • Denver, Colorado

Library of Congress Cataloging-in-Publication Data

Names: Mathuews, Katy B., author. | Harper, Daniel J., author.
Title: Academic library makerspaces : a practical guide to planning, collaborating, and supporting campus innovation / Katy B. Mathuews and Daniel J. Harper.
Description: Santa Barbara, California : Libraries Unlimited, [2020] | Includes bibliographical references and index.
Identifiers: LCCN 2020006101 (print) | LCCN 2020006102 (ebook) | ISBN 9781440872068 (paperback ; acid-free paper) | ISBN 9781440872075 (ebook)
Subjects: LCSH: Makerspaces in libraries. | Academic libraries—Space utilization. | Academic libraries—Planning. | Maker movement in education. | Libraries and colleges.
Classification: LCC Z716.37 .M38 2020 (print) | LCC Z716.37 (ebook) | DDC 025.5—dc23
LC record available at https://lccn.loc.gov/2020006101
LC ebook record available at https://lccn.loc.gov/2020006102

ISBN: 978-1-4408-7206-8 (paperback)
978-1-4408-7207-5 (ebook)

24 23 22 21 20 2 3 4 5 6

This book is also available as an eBook.

Libraries Unlimited
An Imprint of ABC-CLIO, LLC

ABC-CLIO, LLC
147 Castilian Drive
Santa Barbara, California 93117
www.abc-clio.com

This book is printed on acid-free paper ∞

Manufactured in the United States of America

Contents

Introduction

Making has long been recognized as a part of human activity. We make to survive. We also make for pleasure. How we make and where we make have evolved as much as what we make. In recent decades, the invention of new technologies like 3D printers and virtual reality has revolutionized making and invigorated interest in new forms of making. We began to see unique spaces, broadly referred to as makerspaces, created to support this resurgence in making at the turn of the 21st century. Since their appearance up until Lou & Peek's reporting on them in 2016, the number of makerspaces around the globe had reached approximately 1,400. One makerspace of particular significance in this growing movement is the Fab Lab at the Fayetteville Free Library in New York state. The Fab Lab is important not only as an early makerspace in a burgeoning movement but also because it is commonly acknowledged as the first library-based makerspace. Since its opening in 2013, interest in making and makerspaces has continued to skyrocket, with libraries across the country and around the world recognizing the value and logic of makerspaces in libraries.

Our interest in makerspaces and the inspiration for this book were sparked by the opening of one such space in our library. As plans for this space unfolded, we began to study the debates about makerspaces happening everywhere on campus from executive meetings to media reports. We observed the excitement build around the proposed new space as well as the mounting criticisms. We attended open houses for the space and engaged in conversations with everyone from students through administrators. We traveled to and studied other makerspaces across the country and around the world. As the discourse of makerspaces grew, we began to recognize the need to synthesize these experiences and to formalize our learning about makerspaces to benefit others who are or might be engaging in their own makerspace journey.

Three emerging themes in higher education have popularized the practice of making so common in the disciplines of design, architecture, art, and engineering and spread them to other disciplines. First, the desire to break down silos between and among disciplines has made making and the spaces where making happens increasingly popular. For decades, disciplines dove deeper into their own ideas and advanced specialized knowledge. The evolution of knowledge was born out of conversations within disciplines and largely excluded collaboration with other disciplines. The paradigm is shifting. The 21st-century campus is one that embraces collaboration and is witness to the breaking down of silos in favor of inter-, cross-, and multidisciplinary approaches to research as well as teaching and learning. Second, active learning is quickly becoming the model of 21st-century education. Passive learning and the idea that knowledge is transferred from scholar to student are being surpassed by more dynamic and engaging opportunities to learn through discovery and making. Not only are students more invested in active learning, but studies suggest that the end result of active learning is both more effective and more impactful (Bonwell & Eison, 1991). Third, entrepreneurial education has risen to be a priority in much of education today, including postsecondary education. Entrepreneurial education is defined by UNESCO/ILO (2006) as education that seeks to "foster self-esteem and confidence by drawing on the individual's talents and creativity, while building the relevant skills and values that will assist students in expanding their perspectives on schooling and opportunities beyond" (pp. 21–22). Through this definition, contemporary making and makerspaces have become a central component of entrepreneurial education.

What better place for these three themes to intersect than in the academic library? The library has long been seen as neutral territory on campus, a place where all disciplines are welcome and individuals can meet to collaborate without feeling like they are vulnerable outside of their disciplinary home. While some discipline-specific libraries do exist, the academic library is often home to collections and resources representing all disciplines. As a physical place, it represents a nexus of collaboration, active learning, and entrepreneurship. The makerspace, then, becomes a natural evolution of this reality.

The strength of our collaboration on the topic of makerspaces comes from the diversity of our respective backgrounds. Dr. Mathuews is an academic librarian with a diverse background in library functions, including oversight of library budgeting, outreach, instruction, collection development, and curriculum materials center management. Dr. Harper is a design educator with several years of experience as a design practitioner in the area of contract interiors and previously held oversight responsibilities for a campus-based makerspace. Together, we share a background in higher education and the study of student development and organization leadership. This unique combination of education, practice, and experience has enabled us to take both a broad view of and deep dive into the topic of makerspaces.

In the chapters that follow, our goal is to help individuals and organizations understand the makerspace as an emerging reality of the 21st-century academic library. We delve into how to plan for this reality as well as how to maintain it over time as a central component of the overall campus strategy. The book is divided into two parts. In Part I, written by Dr. Harper, we contextualize making and how the design of the academic library makerspace is integral to shifting campus realities. Part I is grounded in establishing an awareness and understanding of making and makerspaces. We share specifics on making as a process and detail the various stages of making as well as the types of makerspaces that might be part of an overall strategy. Likewise, we explore the connection between libraries and makerspaces and establish making as a logical extension of the academic library. Part I includes a very practical approach to planning and maintaining a makerspace in an academic library, and we suggest design thinking as a strategy to help ensure success as part of a planful approach to the makerspace.

In Part II of the book, written by Dr. Mathuews, we shift from establishing awareness and understanding of making and makerspaces and how to plan for and design a makerspace to topics of programming, advocacy, and assessment of the academic library makerspace. Part II provides insight into strategic approaches of connecting the library makerspace to the broader audience of the campus. From event planning to curriculum, Part II is intended to help the reader see and establish the academic library makerspace as an integral component of campus innovation. Likewise, Part II addresses the ever-important topic of advocacy as it relates to initial support but also ongoing and long-term strategy. Part II concludes with the topic of assessment. Closely tied to the design of the space, the programming offered, and how to advocate for makerspaces, assessment strategy is detailed as evidence of how the makerspace is performing against stated visions and missions not only of the makerspace itself, but also as a resource of the library, and as a component of the larger university.

Throughout the book and as evident in the title, we avoid abstract and esoteric approaches to the topic of makerspaces in favor of the pragmatic. Our experiences during the previous few years revealed that individuals and organizations wanted and needed a practical guide. Likewise, we saw the value in a holistic approach to writing a book about makerspaces. Rather than simply focusing on makerspace equipment or providing examples of programming for makerspaces (several great examples of these already exist), we saw value in providing the reader with context, strategy, and tools for the life span of the makerspace endeavor. Our journeys have allowed us to meet individuals and organizations at all stages of planning, implementation, and assessment. Rather than separate volumes addressing each one of these topics, this book offers readers a chance to reflect on their own makerspace and makerspace experiences and to consider and plan for their next step. The essence of innovation is continual evolution. Regardless of what stage you are in with your makerspace, our sharing is intended to support your ongoing efforts.

REFERENCES

Bonwell, C.C. & Eison, J.A. (1991). Active learning: Creating excitement in the classroom. *ASHEERIC Higher Education Report No. 1*, Washington, DC: George Washington University.

Lou, N. & Peek, K. (2016, Feb. 23). By the numbers: The rise of the makerspace. *Popular Science.* Retrieved from https://www.popsci.com/rise-makerspace-by-numbers/

United Nations Educational, Scientific and Cultural Organization (UNESCO)/International Labour Organization (ILO). (2006). *Towards an entrepreneurial culture for the twenty-first century: Stimulating entrepreneurial spirit through entrepreneurship education in secondary schools.* Geneva, Switzerland: ILO/UNESCO.

PART I

Understanding Making and Makerspaces

ONE

Making, Makerspaces, and the Academic Library

Excitement abounds for contemporary making and the emerging tools, equipment, and spaces that support it. This excitement builds on a long history of making. For decades, if not centuries, individuals involved in creative professions from disciplines of art, design, architecture, engineering, and many others have used the process of making as part of their exploration of ideas and as a way to test, revise, and improve outcomes. For artists, designers, and architects, the studio has been the primary place for making. For the engineer, the same holds true for the laboratory. These foundational concepts of place-based making translate to what has become known as the present-day makerspace.

It is fair to say that more recent and still emerging technologies have reinvigorated traditional forms of making. Revolutionary technologies such as 3D printing have opened up a whole new world of making and allowed individuals to quickly, easily, and inexpensively make in ways that have not been possible prior to their advent. These new opportunities in making have challenged us to rethink and perhaps even reimagine the role of making in academia both in creative professions and across the academic landscape. Melo (2019) suggests this is why making matters, because it encourages us to exercise our creative thinking and it prepares individuals to face and solve the problems not only of today but also those of tomorrow.

Beyond the more obvious relationship between makerspaces and the outcomes that originate from them, it is critical to also consider the broader implications of contemporary makerspaces. Making can be positioned as a democratizing tool of contemporary society. The power to leverage making allows individuals and groups to explore new potentials in the form of a do-it-yourself (DIY) approach. If individuals can do it for themselves, they don't have to rely on others to do it for them. This can-do attitude supports increasingly desirable personality characteristics of innovativeness and a spirit of entrepreneurship. Likewise, creative thinking and making allows individuals and small groups to develop ideas that can be scaled into more traditional forms of manufacturing and businesses that have, in recent decades, become increasingly less accessible to those with lesser economic means of starting a business. We also see contemporary making as virtually untethered from traditional gender roles. Where once the type of tool, equipment, or material often dictated who would be doing the making, today's tools, technologies, and spaces for making are idealized as gender neutral.

In the sections that follow, we will explore each of these ideas in more detail and begin to unpack the natural relationship that exists between making and makerspaces and the academic library. We will define making as a process to help you appreciate making in the broader context of tools, technology, and spaces. We will overview the history of making and its connection to education in order to position the contemporary makerspace as an integral part of higher education. Finally, we will discuss why the library is positioned well for making and as a site for makerspaces. While making as a disciplinary practice is not a new concept, the application of making in the broader academic endeavor is. As the first chapter of a practical guide, our intent is to create a foundation of understanding and context for the planning steps that will follow in later chapters.

A CONTEMPORARY DEFINITION OF MAKING

Succinctly, Merriam-Webster defines making as:

1. the act or process of forming, causing, doing, or coming into being
2. a process or means of advancement or success
3. something made, especially a quantity produced at one time
4. potentiality (making)

Perhaps more so than in past traditions of making, the contemporary maker movement emphasizes the process element of Merriam-Webster's definition.

While making is often generalized as simply the action that results in a physical outcome, there are steps and activities both before actual making begins and after an outcome has been realized that comprise the process of making. To illustrate the idea of process and the various steps involved in making, consider the following example as a way of contextualizing process and its various elemental steps.

Let's imagine that you want to make a quilt. This interest likely started with some spark of inspiration. Perhaps you were inspired by a quilt created by someone else: a quilt displayed in a gallery, a quilt you saw in a magazine, or one you came across while surfing the Internet. Perhaps you were inspired to make a quilt out of necessity. A cold winter night found you longing for a warm blanket. Whatever the source, this inspiration will require you to seek out and make material selections and decisions specific to a quilt pattern. You will research your options on both fronts, seeking out just the right combination of material characteristics to pair with a desired pattern for your project. After the quilt top is pieced together, there will be decisions to be made about batting, backing, and how the actual quilting of the various layers will be carried out and how the edges of the quilt will be finished. As you are honing the idea for the quilt, you might also prototype a block to work out the steps of piecing the various parts of the individual quilt block together. This prototype might also test the color and pattern combinations of your selected fabrics. You might practice quilting a sample of the fabric to try different quilting techniques and as an experiment with different threads. Several steps or a process led you up to the actual act of making the quilt. Beyond the quilt itself, you also may be thinking about how the finished quilt will be displayed: on a bed, over the back of a piece of furniture, or perhaps hung on the wall. Part of the making of the quilt will invariably include a self-assessment of your work, reflecting on what you created and how you might do things the same way or differently the next time. You might also put the quilt on display and ask for feedback from others. People who have more experience with any of the steps involved may be able to offer suggestions and insight into your process and its outcome. All of this is intended to inform your next project and will also inform your process the next time. Specific to the actual construction or making of the quilt, consider how and where you will undertake this part of the project. While getting feedback after the fact is helpful, it may also be helpful to create the quilt in a setting with other quilters present. For decades, quilters have gathered to support one another through quilting guilds and have created quilts together in the form of quilting bees.

The free exchange of ideas about quilting and the camaraderie of gathering together to take part in the communal process of making are both helpful and enjoyable to those who take part. Additionally, you may find you do not have the equipment necessary to make a quilt or the space in which to make it. Finding a location that provides both the quilting frame and space for it to be set up will be helpful and necessary.

We use this example to illustrate how making is a process consisting of a series of loosely organized steps. The tradition and process of making apply to a whole range of scenarios from cooking and sewing to creating a PowerPoint or a business plan. In the context of this book, we are focused on making in academia, but, in reality, the process of making and the drivers for it are not unique from one another across the varied project types. Making is not new to us but rather is a reimagined construct of creative thinking and activity applied to 21st-century academic desires and problem-solving.

A TIMELINE OF MAKING

The journey to the present-day maker movement can be traced back across time. Humans have made for as long as they have existed. From early forms of food, clothing, and shelter to the present maker movement, innovation in making has contributed to human survival and thriving. In fact, we might look to the decade of the 1980s as a prime example of this and one that is currently being studied and debated. The 1980s is often considered a turning point in manufacturing in the United States. After decades of innovation in machinery, processes, and techniques, corporate leaders of U.S. industry recognized that they could locate physical making overseas where labor was less regulated and therefore less expensive while maintaining administrative functions in the United States. Some three decades later, we are facing the consequences of such structuring as we begin to recognize the connection between making and survival of a robust economy. We are learning that a healthy economy must support individuals across the employment spectrum, from executives through to actual makers.

For the purposes of this book and with the intent to create context for the history of making here in Chapter 1, we want to highlight some of the milestones in recent history that help us appreciate contemporary making.

1850s—The manual arts become an area of study in the United States. Manual arts focuses on making and fabrication. This is seen as early iterations of contemporary making wherein students focus on the use of hand tools and early machines and common materials of wood and metal, primarily through project-based learning.

1862—Passage of the Morrill Act. Through this act, the federal government codified the importance of making by establishing land-grant institutions to deliver education in the areas of mechanical arts and home economics, among other making-centric disciplines.

1904—Charles R. Richards coins the term "industrial arts education." Replacing the previously popular term of manual training, making is elevated to an art and formalized as education versus rudimentary training.

1976—Apple-1 computer for hobbyists is released. The partnership between Steve Wozniak and Steve Jobs revolutionizes a tradition of computer applications with this introduction of the first personal computer. The personal computer signals the beginning of a transition in making from physical outcomes to digital outcomes.

1980—The term "technology education" replaces "industrial arts education," symbolizing the quick rise in popularity of both computers and their widespread application in teaching and learning; education increasingly incorporates digital making, which largely supplants physical making.

2005—The initial publication of *Make:* magazine. *Make:* is significant not just because it offered do-it-yourself (DIY) projects for individuals but also because it encouraged do-it-with-others (DIWO) projects. This spurred interest in collaborative making and what now might be recognized as the start of the contemporary makerspace movement.

2006—The first Maker Faire is held. Sponsored by *Make:* magazine, the first annual Maker Faire was held at the San Mateo Fairgrounds in San Mateo, California, April 22–23, 2006. During their run, Maker Faires existed as expositions for makers offering workshops, exhibits, competitions, and demonstrations. Maker Faires reinforced both the DIY and DIWO approaches to making, further advancing the makerspace movement.

2013—The first library-based makerspace opens. Known as the Fayetteville Free Library Fab Lab, this makerspace formalized contemporary making in the library and initiated a new era of making and makerspaces.

THE PRECURSOR TO CONTEMPORARY MAKING IN THE LIBRARY

As demonstrated above, making has likewise taken an organic progression in academic libraries. Like other disciplines, libraries have a rich history of hosting spaces for creativity, making, and innovation. Spaces such as audiovisual/technology labs and curriculum materials centers have long found a natural fit in the library setting. Likewise, from the late 20th-century information commons and the early 21st-century learning commons movements to the present-day interest in makerspaces, the library has continually responded to changing patron needs and desires while utilizing technology to advance collaboration, scholarship, and learning. Pushing beyond notions of simply being a repository of resources and information, the library has become a cocurricular space for learning and a space where ideas surface and knowledge is created.

The earlier information commons movement was initially seen as an evolution of the computer lab. With the advent of personal computers, computer labs surfaced as an in-demand resource in libraries. While the interest in computers rose, the cost of owning one was often a limitation for many individuals. As a result, libraries began to carve out space to create information commons to make a valuable yet expensive resource more widely available to both patrons and researchers. Once seen simply as a computer lab, information commons represented a space for ever-expanding associated digital technology. This rapidly expanding digital landscape has influenced how individuals find, evaluate, and use information and as a result, has become a heightened focus of libraries. Likewise, a pedagogical shift from passive to active learning has increased the demand for related technology support and spaces that are designed for collaborative learning. As a result, the notion of a space dedicated to such resources and activities was born in the form of the learning commons (Accardi, Cordova, & Leeder, 2010; Blummer & Kenton, 2017). This access to flexible space and a range of computer technologies saw a blending of traditional library services with complementary nonlibrary services to inform a new vision for the library (Baily & Tierney, 2008). The resulting success of both the information commons and the learning commons movements might be seen as a precursor to the contemporary library-based makerspaces movement. In fact, for some libraries, the makerspace has simply become an offshoot or tangent of the existing learning commons. The idea of once rigid and well-defined spaces within the library is gradually being replaced with notions of spaces that allow for more seamless partnerships between traditionally disparate functions and support collaboration and active learning.

REIMAGING THE LIBRARY FOR THE 21ST CENTURY

Whether willingly or by force, space utilization within the walls of the library proper has changed the character of the academic library and thus the character of the library as a whole. As increasing numbers of patrons see the library as something other than simply books and bookshelves, the library invites in new audiences and potential new types of space usage. The library makerspace as a place for exploration, creativity, and research becomes a natural extension of what the library is or has been doing. The location of a makerspace, either as a library initiative or as an example of a colocation strategy, taps into existing library assets as well as other emerging resources that call the library home.

Collier (2018) and Watters (2011) have suggested that the current embrace of contemporary making by libraries has resulted from a period of library soul-searching. The advent of digital resources and virtual access has led some to question the relevance of the library as a physical place in contemporary society. Additionally, new models of resource sharing among libraries and across library networks have reduced the number of volumes an individual library is required to hold as part of their permanent collection. Even within a library's collection, the use of remote and off-site storage and retrieval systems have reduced the amount and type of square footage a library is required to allocate toward a static collection.

Of course, the notion that libraries are only about physical books is a naïve and narrow one. This disruptive questioning of how we perceive and value libraries has challenged libraries to make their case for relevance and, at the same time, take bold steps in recognizing for themselves how library space is used, why people should come to the library, and reiterate the role of the library in contemporary society to the broader campus community and the surrounding region. Collier (2018) codified this into five strategies intended to strengthen the library's position with the intent of successfully positioning it as part of the academy of the future:

- Establish broad-based processes of community engagement
- Create dynamic, interactive social and educational programming

- Integrate library services with academic methods and practices that reflect the evolving nature of teaching and learning
- Reinforce the librarian's role in the curriculum
- Recapture the serendipitous discoveries of browsing by better understanding digital information production, organization, access, and sharing. (p. 63)

With Collier's strategy in mind, the library-based makerspace becomes an obvious component of this reimaging, hitting on all five points of this future-visioning framework. Library makerspaces, like many library resources, are about community engagement. They invite in makers from all disciplines of the campus community and could be open to the broader regional community of makers. Building on the historically intrinsic connection between libraries and academia, makerspaces are emblematic of active learning, making a library-based makerspace a potentially highly social environment, dynamic in the range of activities happening there. Likewise, depending on how a library-based makerspace is supported, the librarian is poised to be a central figure in helping makers to connect not only with the equipment housed within a given makerspace but also with the resources beyond the walls of the makerspace. Lastly, being located within the library, a library-based makerspace puts makers in the same location as the wealth of other library resources, increasing the likelihood that makers will interact with, either intentionally or by accident, those resources and other collaborative opportunities also found there.

THE LOGIC OF MAKING IN THE LIBRARY

The library has long been seen as a safe place to meet and collaborate. Decades of siloed disciplines have forced would-be collaborators to seek out neutral territory at which to meet, and the library has become just such a space. As researchers see that their inquiries take them into other disciplines, the library becomes a natural place to explore, with physical resources such as books but also a place to engage with experts in other disciplines as in the case of subject librarians. Because of this, it is not uncommon to hear the library referred to as an important Third Place on campus. Oldenburg (1997), in his study of the phenomenon known as the Third Place, is solid grounding for understanding the value of the library and why it might also be the optimal location for a makerspace. He suggests that the Third Place is often and wrongly characterized as simply the other place, a "haven of escape from home and work" (p. 22). Such a definition reveals little about why such a space is actually valuable and what it offers to those who repeatedly use it. Instead, Oldenburg delves deeper into defining and describing true Third Place scenarios framed by eight characteristics that partner nicely with desirable makerspace characteristics. Oldenburg's eight characteristics include space that exists as neutral ground, provides leveling specific to skills and abilities, the presence of conversation, access and accommodation, patrons comprised of regulars, a low-profile existence, playfulness, and a sense of home away from home.

Neutral Ground

Primary to creating a successful Third Place is the idea that it can be entered and left freely. Individuals are not locked into a specific form of engagement or committed by time but rather are free to come and go as they feel compelled to do so. Qualifiers of time, productivity, or commitment are not used to qualify individuals who enter a Third Place. In the context of the library makerspace, the ability for individuals to simply drop in and tinker with something and then leave makes for an ideal Third Place scenario. Freedom from pressures of schedules, counts, or quality control make the library makerspace an ideal Third Place for individuals.

Leveling

In contemporary lingo, we might refer to the idea of the Third Place as being inclusive. Here the concept is that everyone is equal once they enter the library/makerspace and that pretense and prestige are left at the door. It is important to note that certainly there are different proficiency levels with equipment and process, but in the case of a makerspace that successfully functions as a leveler, individuals feel welcome and able to communicate and work across those lines of distinction. In many ways, this is seen as more of an attitude that individuals adopt rather than leveling up in terms of skills or abilities.

Conversation

The Third Place is marked by the primary activity of conversation rather than outcome or production. The success of a Third Place is often noted by the level of communication that happens across groups and between individuals in a makerspace. In Chapter 2, we will introduce various spaces that might be associated with makerspaces, one of which is the lounge. In the later discussion of the lounge, we will draw from Oldenburg's (1997) belief in the power of conversation in creating a successful makerspace vis-à-vis the Third Place framework. Providing spaces that are conducive to conversation creates powerful Third Place scenarios. This is also one of the primary struggles of the makerspace as a Third Place because such conversations must first be valued. When creating the plan for a makerspace in the library, it must be recognized why places for casual conversation are important. Likewise, we must be good at such forms of conversation. Conversation ensues when individuals have something to talk about, some commonality. In many ways, makers self-select into makerspaces because of this. Makers may drop into a Third Place makerspace because they know other makers will be there or the curiosity about making lures individuals in with an expectation of leveling up on making.

Access and Accommodation

Individuals go to makerspaces when they know they will be accessible and when the makerspace provides for things makers desire. Making does not happen on a schedule but rather is often an impromptu activity when inspiration strikes the maker. If the desire is for the library makerspace to be a Third Place, hours of operation will have to be considered along with how those hours accommodate making before, during, or after other activities happening on campus. Just as the hours of the library's learning commons are often extended, the makerspace hours will need to be as well if it is intended to draw similar crowds. This point will be explored further in Chapter 3 in terms of practical planning considerations.

Regulars

Oldenburg (1997) suggests that the equipment and services notwithstanding, what will support ongoing attraction of individuals to a library makerspace will be the other patrons. As a Third Place, familiarity is key in creating a comfortable and inviting space. Having regular patrons in the space makes for easier conversations and aids in the leveling capabilities of a space. If patrons become familiar with each other and those that operate a makerspace, they are more likely to return and feel part of it as a Third Place rather than viewing the makerspace from a task-driven perspective.

In Chapter 3, we report more on this in terms of how a makerspace is staffed and operated.

Low Profile

Oldenburg (1997) also suggests that a key characteristic of Third Place success is that it operates at a low profile. This may be counter to the desires of those investing hundreds of thousands if not millions of dollars in the design of a makerspace. The belief here is that high-profile spaces suggest a pressure to perform and focuses attention on outcomes, ultimately steering people away from makerspaces rather than attracting them. Likewise, the suggestion of plainness supports earlier goals of spaces that feel accessible and welcoming. If makers have to become or appear as something other than what they are, the makerspace as a Third Place is likely to be less successful. In Chapter 3, we discuss ideas of privacy for makers and how the feeling of being onstage has possible implications on making.

Playful

Oldenburg (1997) found that spaces that maintained a playful attitude and exuded a playful character were more successful Third Places. The library-based makerspace supports this character in that it is remote from disciplinary oversight. The pressure to perform within disciplinary boundaries is removed when making in a library. Likewise, begin to think about how the things that are made enhance the sense of playfulness. You will notice that the 3D printer filament, for example, comes in colors that are bright and playful. Pipe cleaners and LEGOs in tinkerspaces likewise come in colorful options and allow for simple, playful exploration. Likewise, the objects that can be downloaded and readily printed from Thingiverse run the gamut of sophistication, but nothing is more playful than 3D printing toys or animals and putting them on display and making them available in a Thingiverse toybox.

Home Away from Home

Oldenburg (1997) suggests that Third Places succeed when they feel like a home away from home. Individuals are as comfortable in the Third Place makerspace as they are at home. In Chapter 3, we will discuss design strategy as part of the library makerspace planning, but here it is important to note that individuals must be comfortable and at ease in the makerspace for it to function as a successful Third Place. Beyond furniture, materials, and finishes, the people (regulars) within a makerspace help to create the spirit of home, which attracts individuals to the makerspace as a Third Place. Likewise, the degree to which Third Places are able to function as levelers contributes to the homelike qualities that makers are attracted to, as discussed earlier.

As with other Third Place scenarios such as coffee shops, bars, and community centers, there are qualities about both the library and the makerspace within that support makers in feeling like they belong. This sense of belonging then inspires makers to go to these Third Places as making destinations. Beyond Oldenburg's (1997) Third Place characteristics, though, the library is imbued with a number of intentional and unintentional characteristics that result from activities and programming that happen in the library. Whether the result of library initiatives or simply happening by chance, these characteristics should also be recognized as part of what makes the library a logical place to locate a makerspace.

Location

The library is often centrally located on campus. This planning tradition symbolizes the long-standing belief that libraries are at the heart of academia. Physically locating libraries in such a way reinforces this belief and provides equitable access to the library to all members of the campus community. To this point, Provenzano (2016) offers several helpful suggestions specific to potential locations for a makerspace as well as warning about places to avoid. While we will elaborate on this topic in future chapters, the important thing to consider here is how the existing location of a library likely offers several benefits of access to patrons. This same logic of access can be applied to makerspaces. If making is part of or intended to be part of an institutional mission, the central location of a library makes it a potentially ideal location for colocating a makerspace within.

Likewise, we might think of the location of the library in philosophical terms. Here we mean that the library is thought to go hand in hand with learning and research. When you imagine the campus, you naturally think of or possibly picture the library as part of the image. The stereotypical books and study carrels of the library are as much a part of our image of higher education as the graduation cap and gown. Making the makerspace part of this image helps to solidify making as part of academia.

Tradition

Willingham & De Boer (2015) point out that libraries have always been a place of making, "making knowledge, building insight, and launching investigations into the nature of things" (p. 1). In this tradition, the authors suggest that libraries are not only a natural fit for makerspaces but that they should "become an active source of skills acquisition and productivity" (p. 1). Graves, Graves, & Rendina (2017) expand on this idea and suggest that thinking about making in the library is less about physical space and more about a shift in conceptualizing what making is and what it means for both the library and the patron. Making and its various forms should be thought of simply as an extension of what is already happening in the library and should be leveraged to build upon the existing assets of the library.

Collections

Bagley (2014) reminds us that the library is made up of innumerable resources and collections to support patrons and the needs of researchers. A makerspace should be considered an extension of this idea. Whether it is a collection of tools, equipment, or spaces, a library-based makerspace can be conceptualized as yet another collection, offering makers access to resources that may otherwise be out of reach to some or all patrons. Just as existing library patrons often rely on the library for access to books and journals, makers will rely on the library-based makerspace for access to potentially expensive equipment and a range of tools that they either cannot afford or do not have the space for. In this way, we might also consider the ideological framing of equitable access to such resources as furthering the democratic mission of libraries. As Kranich (2001) notes, "libraries serve the most fundamental ideals of our society as uniquely democratic institutions" (p. vi). We rely on libraries to provide access to a whole range of resources that we otherwise would not have.

Hospitality

Collier (2018) suggests that the library has become a casual campus center as much as it is a library in the traditional sense of books and bookshelves. For decades, students who commute to campus rather than reside on campus have sought out the library as a landing spot. On many campuses, the library has become one of the few places to study, relax, and wait, before and after class meeting times and for times between classes. This fact has already made the library a popular site for colocation initiatives such as academic advising, tutoring, writing centers, and many other student-facing initiatives. As a result, the makerspace is a natural extension of this concept.

Outreach

Beyond the commuter student focus, central to the mission of the library has been outreach. For students generally, the library is often seen as hosting events to support student life. From study break activities during exam weeks to hosting social events during parent and sibling visit weekends, the library is increasingly seen for its hospitality to the broader campus. Outreach also extends to the surrounding community, with the library often hosting author talks and readings and exhibitions targeting the campus community but also extending its audience to members of the surrounding community and region. Because of this, the library already exists as the kind of place where makerspaces thrive and to which patrons are attracted.

These ideas begin to offer insight into why locating a makerspace in a library is a logical strategy for both the library and for the larger institution. In reality, making is already happening in the library and it may be helpful to simply refresh this thinking into a broader, more expansive view of contemporary making and ideas about the potential for a formal makerspace in the library. To be sure, we have only scratched the surface here specific to this logic, but our intent is to inspire your thinking on this topic.

CONCLUSION

Making is intrinsically tied to who we are as individuals and how we exist as a society. While making has evolved in recent years to include exciting new equipment, technology, and spaces, making is not new. We have been makers from the very beginning as part of human survival and human evolution. With these realities in mind, we can then begin to appreciate making as a formalized process. While experiencing periods of heightened attention and waning enthusiasm, making has been ingrained in the educational system of the United States. Over time, it has been given different names to describe the process, yet, at its heart, we have taught making as a central part of our educational values.

Likewise, the logic of making in the library exists as a long-standing tradition that has also evolved over time to take on different forms. Our goal for this chapter was to create context for both making, generally, and making in the library, specifically. Our hope is that by contextualizing making in this way, you feel more comfortable with ideas of making and makerspaces but also feel empowered to advocate for and plan a makerspace. In the chapters that follow, we will continue in this direction, offering increasingly specific details to help in the practical planning of a library-based makerspace.

ADDITIONAL READINGS

Dewey, J. (2010). *Democracy and education: An introduction to the philosophy of education*. Memphis, TN: General Books.

Fernandez, P.D. & Tilton, K. (eds.). (2018). *Applying library values to emerging technology*. Chicago, IL: Association of College and Research Libraries.

Gorman, M. (2015). *Our enduring values revisited: Librarianship in an ever-changing world*. Chicago, IL: ALA Editions.

Hodge, A. & Zwaan, B. (2006). *Risen: Why libraries are here to stay. The technology that almost took the library's power away is now giving it back*. Amsterdam, The Netherlands: Medialab Solutions.

REFERENCES

Accardi, M.T., Cordova, M., & Leeder, K. (2010). Reviewing the library learning commons: History, models, and perspectives. *College & Undergraduate Libraries, 17*(2–3), 310–329.

Bagley, C. (2014). *Makerspaces: Top trailblazing projects*. Chicago, IL: American Library Association.

Bailey, D.R. & Tierney, B.G. (2008). *Transforming library service through information commons: Case studies for the digital age.* Chicago, IL: American Library Association.

Blummer, B. & Kenton, J.M. (2017). Learning commons in academic libraries: Discussing themes in the literature from 2001 to the present. *New Review of Academic Librarianship, 23*(4), 329–352.

Collier, N. (2018, Oct.-Dec.). Change and renewal for existing campus libraries: Success strategies and lessons learned. *Planning for Higher Education Journal, 47*(1), 63–75.

Graves, C., Graves, A., & Rendina, D.L. (2017). *Challenge-based learning in the school library makerspace.* Santa Barbara, CA: Libraries Unlimited.

Kranich, N. (2001). *Libraries & democracy: The cornerstones of liberty.* Chicago, IL: American Library Association.

Making. Retrieved from https://www.merriam-webster.com/dictionary/making

Melo, M. (2019, July). The possibilities and perils of inclusion in makerspaces. Keynote address at the Makerspaces for Innovation and Research in Academics (MIRA) Conference. La Verne, CA.

Oldenburg, R. (1997). *The great good place.* New York, NY: Marlowe & Company.

Provenzano, N. (2016). *Your starter guide to makerspaces.* Blend Education.

Watters, A. (2011, Nov. 9). The public library, completely reimagined. *Mindshift.* Retrieved from https://www.kqed.org/mindshift/16781/the-public-library-completely-reimagined

Willingham, T. & De Boer, J. (2015). *Makerspaces in libraries.* Lanham, MD: Rowman & Littlefield.

TWO

Design Thinking and the Organization of Making and Makerspaces

In Chapter 1, we offered a definition of making and contextualized makerspaces in libraries. We revealed the natural relationship between libraries and makerspaces that helps to explain the library-based makerspace movement. In Chapter 2, we dive deeper. In the sections that follow, we begin by offering an overview of design thinking as a planning strategy. As you begin to think about planning a makerspace, using a design thinking approach will help to ensure a successful end result. We then move into specifics about different types of spaces where making happens. Casually, individuals often default to the term *makerspace*, but here we offer specific vocabulary identifying types of making spaces as defined by the making that takes place within each type. We go on to position makerspaces in the broader context of a campus-wide ecosystem of making, and further, we provide an overview of basic organizational models of makerspaces as they relate to that ecosystem. We also feel it is important to understand makerspaces by way of the people who make in them. To this end, we conclude Chapter 2 with a discussion of the people in makerspaces.

Our goal in Chapter 2 is to lay out the options for how you might begin to imagine a makerspace in your library and how such a space might be positioned either as a stand-alone opportunity or as part of a broader network of making. This chapter is intended to give you the background and foundation of understanding to then, in Chapter 3, embrace more pragmatic planning and design of a makerspace.

DESIGN THINKING

There are numerous philosophies that inspire what and how we design, largely attempting to answer the big question of whether the built environment is proactive or reactive to activity. The implication, then, is that it is important to consider whether we create spaces that influence our behavior—what we do and how we act—or whether we create spaces that respond to our behaviors—the shape and form of spaces we create being a reflection of our behaviors and activities. To bring this idea home, you might think of your own kitchen. Does your kitchen influence how and what you make in that space, or do your desires to make certain things in the kitchen influence how you adjust and alter the kitchen to make it work for you? Winston Churchill, commenting on the relationship between the built environment and its occupants, once famously said, "we shape our buildings, and afterward, our buildings shape us" (Parliament, n.d.). This insight continues to be true even today. In reality, a good makerspace design should be both. It should provide opportunities in response to demand, but it should also offer things that make us curious and allow for new exploration in ways we had perhaps not imagined.

As you embark on creating a makerspace in your library, you will have to wrestle with these ideas. It is easy to get caught up in an equipment list and allow that list to drive the design of space. If the demand for technology is the impetus for your makerspace, then that approach may work out fine for you. If, on the other hand, you are thinking about how technology might enhance teaching and learning and you have specific outcome goals in mind, you may want to start with a different list in a process known as design thinking. In essence, with the desired end goals in mind, back up from there through the planning process to ensure that what you ultimately desire from the space helps to foster the planning of it. In the section that follows, we elaborate on this approach and offer an overview of design thinking and how to apply it in the planning of a makerspace.

Design Thinking as a Planning Strategy

In *Design Thinking: Process and Methods Manual*, Curedale (2013) offers three points in defining design thinking as a planning process. These points align perfectly with the planning of a makerspace. First, Curedale states that design thinking is a people-centered process. A people-centered approach to planning places makers at the center of the planning process. It considers how makers will utilize the space to both make and collaborate. This is a key consideration in a design thinking approach to planning makerspaces. The excitement about equipment can easily overshadow the needs of makers in a makerspace. When this happens, you will often see makerspaces that go underutilized or equipment sitting idle.

Second, Curedale states that design thinking is "a team-based process which is cross disciplinary and collaborative" (p. 13). Later in this chapter and also in Chapter 3, we will share more specifics on the idea of collaboration and elaborate on the various partners who may be part of the planning and design process. As well, we will offer insight into understanding makers as individuals within a makerspace, and we will discuss the role of managers and employees, all of whom should be part of a collaborative planning process in accordance with a design thinking approach.

Third, Curedale states that design thinking "seeks practical and innovative solutions to problems" (p. 13). Do not let the phrase "solutions to problems" scare you, as this may be somewhat misleading and cause undue stress. Makerspaces are broadly seen as opportunities, not problems, to enhance academics and expand the potential of research. We would encourage you to avoid framing the planning of a makerspace as a problem and to focus primarily on Curedale's "practical and innovative" component of this third point. Consider the planning of a makerspace and the chance to use design thinking as an opportunity to learn about something new and expand your knowledge base. The goal of design thinking is to make the planning process both thoughtful and methodical, ideally allaying frustration on the part of those who embark on the planning process. To this point, later in this chapter we introduce a typology of makerspaces to help define a basic structure of understanding about what, how, and where making happens. We also introduced basic organizational structures of the making ecosystem. The reality is that even within the confines of those descriptions, there is great variability. This is not the definition of a problem but rather an opportunity to tailor the space to specific needs and wants of the various patrons of a space with diverse interests in making.

A makerspace is different than any other space in the library, but it shares a common set of characteristics and qualities inherent to a library. In Chapter 5, we elaborate further on this point and share how to conceptualize a mission and vision for a makerspace that supports the mission and vision of both the library it resides in and the broader university. The makerspace function, the resources housed within, and how it will be utilized may not be familiar to everyone in the library, though. Because of this, an innovative planning process that engages the design thinking approach will help to ensure a successful outcome.

The Design Thinking Process

Makerspaces can and often have evolved organically in a sort of "build it and they will come" approach. This approach is less formal. Physical space might simply be designated for making without a plan to intentionally guide its development. Tools and equipment might be donated or cobbled together based on individual interest or by a casual group of organizers. This type of approach can certainly be successful but, because of its informal structure, tends to be narrower in focus and typically supports a very specific audience. Conversely, a design thinking approach can be used to initiate a much more formal approach to planning and design of a makerspace. The latter relies on an intentional strategy born out of a deep dive into understanding. A design thinking approach assesses both individual needs and desires but also considers library and institutional interest in making tied to academic goals. As a formal and intentional approach to planning, design thinking is iterative and happens in five stages or steps: empathizing, defining, ideating, prototyping, and testing. These steps can be revisited or undertaken more than once until the solutions are found and a strategy is agreed upon. These five stages are described below.

Empathizing

In this stage, the intent is to gain an understanding of possible goals (or problems) of makers. This happens through any number of qualitative or quantitative methods from observations and interviews to surveys and questionnaires. The process may reveal insight into how makers make, what they make, where they prefer to make, what tools they use in the making process, and what their outcomes are. It may also reveal what makers need or want that they do not already have, what is holding them back, and what is stifling creativity. As the researcher, you are engaging in a process of discovery about making. Again, making is not easily defined as a single activity, process, or outcome, so empathizing with your maker population is important to assess their needs versus making assumptions. Beyond makers, engage with the broader population of constituents. If, for example, faculty are interested in either curricular or cocurricular making, begin to think about how a library makerspace might support this and inquire as to what exactly this might look like to faculty. Likewise, if administrators want to promote entrepreneurship on campus, strive to understand what they mean by this. For some this could mean supporting individuals in business start-ups; for others it could mean product development leading to patents. These two desires need very different types of support in a makerspace. Additionally, consider reaching out to future employers of graduates of the institution. Assess what they are looking for and what kinds of making activities they would find impressive and desirable in those graduates. The various vendors of makerspace equipment and resources may also be of help. The makerspace you are planning is not the first, so equipment vendors may be able to offer insight into earlier success or failures.

Defining

Once there is a rich sense of empathy, begin to define what exactly the goals will be for your makerspace. You will likely not be able to address every need or want that was discovered from the first stage of design thinking. Because of this it is important to have a clear definition of what your makerspace is intended to address or accomplish, and how. A clear and succinct definition of goals will help to ensure success by creating direction for the planning process. At the same time, clear definitions help to get everyone involved in the planning on the same page. As you define, strive to be people focused. If no one shows up to use the equipment in a makerspace, all you have is a room full of equipment. At the same time, focus on positive outcomes rather than negative realities. Define what is possible rather than how you are limited. For example, your institution might have identified the goal of helping to strengthen the local economy; a definition of intent or purpose might then be:

> "*Not enough business start-ups succeed to sustain the economy.*"

This is neither people focused nor positive. Rather, frame the same observation from the empathizing stage as both positive and people focused:

> "*We want to support students in turning their ideas for businesses into a reality and thereby support the local economy.*"

By doing this, right away you are inviting others to begin to imagine how to support students and helping people become curious about what kinds of businesses students are dreaming up. When you codify both a direction and goals in a people-focused, positive manner, others can agree to this by registering support or disagree by registering concern. Either way, you begin to develop a sense of direction that has meaning.

Ideating

Once you have defined the goals for the makerspace, the next step is to think about ways to achieve those goals. In the scenario above of supporting students, you can begin to imagine the ways to support them and their ideas. This could happen by granting students access to specific equipment and resources. It could happen by developing a mentoring program where faculty or visiting entrepreneurs partner with students in the makerspace to work on their ideas. It could mean that the makerspace needs to offer meeting rooms or collaboration space. During the ideation stage, include a diverse group of collaborators to develop ideas. Different perspectives result in diverse solutions. Likewise, disqualify naysayers. In the ideation stage, all ideas are valid and represent a potential direction. At this stage, ideation is about casting a wide net and capturing all of the ideas and then whittling them down to the most likely to succeed or most feasible given existing parameters. Ideation is supported by a range of activities intended to foster big, broad idea generation: brainstorming, sketching, and the SCAMPER approach. SCAMPER is an acronym for substitute, combine, adjust, modify, put to use, eliminate, and reverse. The idea here is to look at and rearrange an idea to generate more and more ideas. The result of ideation can take many forms, anything from equipment and amenities lists to ideas about how the space might be planned and designed. Ideally, ideation is fun and satisfying.

From ideation, engage in a democratic voting process to identify the best ideas to move forward. For example, each collaborator in the design thinking process might receive three votes to identify their top three favorite ideas. Once voting has concluded, the three ideas with the greatest number of votes are moved into the prototyping stage.

Prototyping

Prototyping means that some version of the idea is put into action. Back to the original idea of supporting students in starting businesses, if a winning idea is to provide students with meeting space within the makerspace, then the next step is to try some initial version of this. Convert a portion of the intended makerspace into a meeting room. Through prototyping you are able to test the size of the meeting space, the type and configuration of furniture, and any of a host of other components or planning strategies for the meeting space. If mocking up the actual space is not feasible, consider an alternative of preparing drawings of the proposed space. This is often more cost-effective but perhaps not as informative. A good rule of thumb is to consider more authentic exploration of ideas for those things that will be more costly to implement. You want to be sure the idea is solid before investing a lot of time and money into something that may not pan out. From here, you move into the final stage of design thinking, which is testing.

Testing

Once the prototype meeting space has been created, grant students access to it and test its effectiveness. Watch to see if and how the meeting spaces are being used. Ask students their opinions about the meeting spaces and how they are helpful and how they might be improved. Be sure to allow enough time for testing to ensure accurate test results. Likewise, if you are not mocking up the actual space but rather presenting drawings of the proposed spaces, be sure the drawings are on display long enough for individuals to review and consider them. As above, you do not want to rush through this stage only to find that testing was unsuccessful because of time constraints.

As testing concludes, this is an opportunity to reflect on the learning from the process. Consider the success or lack thereof for the three ideas originally tested. The measure of success results from comparing observed behavior of students using the spaces against the desired behaviors. If you are seeing students favor one space over the others, or if students report positively about the potential of one design over the others, you begin to gauge the success of the design proposals. Once the prototype(s) are deemed successful, move into actual implementation; or, if they were not a success, circle back around and revise the original in response to test findings or select new ideas to prototype and test.

Again, design thinking is an iterative process. Ultimately, it is intended to ensure success through a collaboration of diverse constituents toward a common goal that has been researched, vetted, and tested. Design thinking helps to ensure that resources are allocated toward proven outcomes and intends to eliminate wasted investment in untested ideas. Referring back to Curedale's three points of design thinking as a process, the example above illustrates how to position people at the center of the process, how to make the process collaborative, and how the process solves a problem or creates a feasible direction toward an opportunity.

A Typology of Spaces for Making

As part of the exploration of makerspaces, it is helpful to recognize that there is a vocabulary associated with the maker movement specific to different types of spaces dedicated to making. These making spaces are defined by the activities and processes that happen in these spaces that is largely informed by the presence, or lack, of technology. You may find some of the vocabulary quite valuable as a way of defining activities happening within a particular space. Likewise, you may find other parts of the vocabulary peculiar and clearly borrowed from unrelated industries, albeit helpful in creating understanding. For example, the terms *incubator* and *hatchery* are part of the language of making yet are clearly borrowed from the poultry industry. How these ended up as maker vocabulary is unknown, but the descriptions are helpful in understanding the intent of the various spaces. Consider this borrowing of words to be part of the joy and cleverness of the making culture.

For clarity, we will present key terms in this section to serve as an introduction. Some individuals and organizations use these descriptors interchangeably in a generic manner similar to identifying a facial tissue as a Kleenex versus using Kleenex as a brand name. You will find that other individuals are steadfast and adhere to a strict vocabulary that they find to be key in differentiating spaces and as helpful in recognizing how a particular space is tied to a specific manner of making and physical outcomes.

Makerspace

Starting with the term makerspace, it is generally accepted that it is broadly applied to any space where making happens. Regardless of processes, tools, or outcomes, a makerspace simply suggests that individuals or groups are engaged in a process of producing a digital or physical outcome. From the American Library Association's TechSource, Bagley (2013) defined makerspaces succinctly as "a place where people come together to create with technology." The title makerspace suggests an outcome resulting from the combination or compilation of disparate parts. This concept evolved from hackerspaces, which is more specifically defined later but generally suggests the opposite, hacking things into parts. Making then becomes the result of first hacking things into pieces and then assembling those pieces into a new composition or starting with elemental parts to construct something more complex. Because of the range of spaces that fall under the heading of makerspace, we feature three here to help illustrate the similarities and differences that may exist across the definition of makerspace.

Featured Makerspace: American University's Bender Library Makerspace

Describing the makerspace as "a place where people with similar interests can come together to work on projects while sharing ideas and knowledge," which "facilitates the construction of knowledge through the manipulation and creation of material objects" (American University, n.d.), Bender Library's makerspace offers a range of tools, equipment, and spaces in which to make. Making activities are divided across three broad categories of 3D creation (see Figure 2.1), craft fabrication (see Figure 2.2), and digital production (see Figure 2.3). While the tools and equipment are grouped together to support each category of making, the makerspace might best be described as a generally open environment with designated benches or clustered activities rather than physically separated spaces.

Figure 2.1 Makerspace 3D creation space.

Figure 2.2 Makerspace craft fabrication space.

Figure 2.3 Makerspace digital production space.

Featured Makerspace: The University of Sydney's ThinkSpace

Described as "a technology-driven, creative play-space that provides you with the opportunity to collaborate, design and create interesting things using new technologies" (The University of Sydney, n.d.), ThinkSpace has designated areas for making, but the makerspace, as a whole, is largely open, with segregated activities that meld into each other (see Figure 2.4). Designated areas within ThinkSpace include 3D production, a recording studio (one of the enclosed spaces, separate from other making activities for acoustic purposes), a virtual reality space and related equipment, and a digital design area with a suite of computers and design software. Likewise, ThinkSpace includes a central collaborative area made up of mobile tables and chairs.

Figure 2.4 The University of Sydney's ThinkSpace (Namibian elephants photographs by Antonia Mocatta).

Featured Makerspace: Carnegie Mellon's IDeATe@Hunt Making Facility

Carnegie Mellon University describes the IDeATe making facility as supporting "students and faculty working together across disciplines in maker experiences that combine arts and technology. These types of collaborative, learning-through-making experiences are a key part of the residential experience at Carnegie Mellon, where experts from diverse areas with curious, open minds meet to develop the next great ideas. Students involved in such experiences have the opportunity to expand their collaborate innovation skills and cognitive versatility. Through these experiences students are also prepared to address the growing demand for collaborative professionals in the creative industries, such as social media, game design, and responsive environments. The placement of the facility in the Hunt Library signifies the evolution of the library into a mediated learning commons, where students can evolve diverse media literacy and their ability to learn and communicate through new media" (n.d.).

In the case of IDeATe, the making spaces are divided into discrete areas for digital fabrication, a computing lab (see Figure 2.5), an area for interactive media, and space for more traditional fabrication. Additionally, IDeATe includes collaboration space in the form of a classroom.

Figure 2.5 Carnegie Mellon's IDeATe@Hunt making facility.

We feature these three makerspaces to illustrate the similarities across makerspaces specific to activities, tools, and equipment. While the size of each makerspace varies, you begin to see how the designation of activities results in the clustering of tools and equipment around specific making activities and processes in each of the three featured makerspaces. It is safe to say this is common practice across the spectrum of makerspaces. Since we are early in the library-based makerspace movement, it is not uncommon to see space for a makerspace simply carved out of existing space. This may result in some makerspaces being more segregated, with tools and equipment being separated into existing rooms or spaces while other libraries may have funding to redesign space to allow for less segregation of activities, leaning toward the open plan concept for a makerspace. In Chapter 3, we will dive deeper into important planning considerations regardless of which scenario you are dealing with. This quote from American University's Bender Library sums it up nicely: "Makerspaces come in all shapes and sizes but they all serve as a gathering point for tools, projects, mentors and expertise. A collection of tools does not define a Makerspace. Rather we define it by what it enables: a community of making" (American University, n.d.).

Hackspace, Hackerspace, or Hack Lab

The term *hackerspace* is often used interchangeably with the more familiar term makerspace even though it is recognized in the maker community to be unique from a makerspace. A hackerspace implies more rudimentary approaches to making, as in "hacking away" at something or "hacking into" something to gain access. It is often a space where building components are first scavenged or harvested from existing objects with the intent of creating something out of those harvested parts. An example of making in a hackerspace would be to construct a computer out of computer parts recycled from an existing computer(s) that had been disassembled. The original computer was hacked apart, and then those parts were recycled into a newly assembled computer. It is important to note that the more contemporary appreciation of hacking as in security hacking or Internet-based hacking is not the type of activity associated with a hackerspace founded on the goals of making in the maker movement.

Fabrication Laboratory, or Fab Lab

Similar to a hackerspace, a fab lab is often used generically to refer to a makerspace and vice versa. The concept of a fab lab, though, is grounded in technology-based making and suggests more sophisticated processes, techniques, and outcomes. While the term makerspace often triggers thoughts of 3D printers, fab labs might be better understood to start with 3D printers but to elevate the quality and abilities of the equipment from basic prototyping to more advanced machining and milling of manufacturable products, perhaps more sophisticated software, and generally a stronger design focus and outcome. At the same time, a fab lab setup might shy away from more rudimentary forms of making that might be more common to either a hackerspace or a properly defined makerspace.

Due to their nature of specialization and sophistication related to making, fab labs, in their truest sense, are not a typical type found in a library but rather are more commonly found in discipline-specific spaces where the need for specific tools and equipment for advanced making are more commonly desired.

Tinkerspace

On the opposite end of the spectrum, a *tinkerspace* is recognized as having less sophisticated equipment and processes than those found in fab labs and other makerspaces. Tinkerspaces are intentionally more rudimentary in nature and light on, if not devoid of, technology in an effort to invite free and open thinking about ideas and the potential of making. While some in the maker movement see tinkerspaces as outside of the realm of the makerspace label, adhering to Bagley's definition of making with technology, tinkering is often the precursor of formalized making and can involve common supplies such as popsicle sticks, pipe cleaners, and even LEGOs as building blocks of basic making.

Stand-Alone Resources

In the context of broadly defined makerspaces described in the section above, it is important to also recognize and acknowledge that not all making has evolved to the point of commanding its own dedicated space with an extensive array of tools and making equipment. For some institutions, early forays into making might exist as a single 3D printer situated on a tabletop near a reference desk. While perhaps not recognized as a makerspace in the purest sense, making is still happening and it occupies space, albeit limited. It is important to recognize this reality as such making often evolves into more formal spaces and serves as a conduit for makers to engage in alternative modes of making beyond hand tools or virtual resources. Additionally, the passion for making is no less diminished in such scenarios. It is thus valid to honor stand-alone resources for their support of making activities.

In terms of intent, stand-alone making may be interpreted in number of ways, for example. The stand-alone 3D printer may be intended to introduce students to 3D printing at a very elementary level, perhaps by granting them access to a basic 3D printer that is used to print off 3D models from a virtual library. An example might be that students come to a stand-alone 3D printer and select a keychain to print from a collection of three different models. In this case, the intent is to expose students to the wonder of 3D printers and spark curiosity. Alternatively, a stand-alone scenario may exist on the opposite end of the spectrum. In this case, featuring a more advanced 3D printer gives individuals who have greater printing experience and needs access to a potentially expensive piece of equipment. In this second scenario, it becomes a sort of print-on-demand opportunity. Both scenarios suggest a rather hands-off approach to management of the making. The use of the equipment is self-directed and can be supported by basic, on-site instructions.

Featured Makerspace: University of Washington, Tacoma's Learning and Research Commons

Described as "a service by the Library to support the coursework of UW Tacoma's students" and "to help build a maker community on campus by allowing students to learn about maker technologies like the 3D printer in a peer-taught environment" (University of Washington, Tacoma, n.d.), the 3D printing station is an excellent example of a stand-alone making resource. Stand-alone making differs from other sorts of makerspace organization in both scale and intent. In this scenario, stand-alone making adheres to three basic principles: focus, independence, and ease of access. Stand-alone making may exist separate from other making activities, in the mode of segregated making. It represents focused attention on a specific form of making, in this case 3D printing. Lastly, stand-alone making is also often intended to be easily accessible in a sort of walk-up, self-serve approach. In the Learning and Research Commons at the University of Washington, Tacoma, the 3D printer is located on a tabletop along a major thruway with no other making equipment in the vicinity (see Figure 2.6). It may be overseen by someone in the general vicinity, but it is often not the sole focus for any individual to manage.

Figure 2.6 University of Washington, Tacoma's Learning and Research Commons.

Sandbox

Sandbox is a term commonly used in instructional design to describe a space dedicated to testing or experimenting with new ideas, tools, and equipment intended to enhance teaching and learning. In the context of makerspaces, this is a unique scenario. A sandbox is generally recognized more as a teaching and learning space rather than a making space, yet making does happen.

Focused on pedagogy, a sandbox is intended for faculty, staff, and graduate student research and development versus ongoing making. Individuals might go to a sandbox to test a specific piece of equipment or a process before introducing it to a class as an activity or assignment. They might meet with instructional designers to talk about a specific learning outcome or goal and be looking for a way to incorporate making to meet that outcome or goal. Likewise, faculty, staff, and graduate students might reach out to the individuals who oversee a sandbox and discuss the potential of specific equipment in a new pedagogical strategy. Through this collaboration, equipment might be purchased for a sandbox for testing purposes. The equipment then becomes yet another resource available to individuals in the sandbox to explore and test.

A sandbox is often not a making destination but rather a testing ground for ideas. We offer it here because it can often look like and function as a form of makerspace. A sandbox may be located in a library along with other faculty, staff, and graduate student spaces related to teaching and learning research and development opportunities.

Collectively, consider the scenarios described above as existing on a continuum of spaces designed for making. Individually, each type of space provides a range of tools, relies on unique sets of processes, and aims for diverse outcomes. From stand-alone resources to spaces dedicated to advanced fabrication, regardless of how you use the terms above, making is happening as a result of creative exploration and in the attempt to uncover new ideas and solutions to some set of proposed parameters or problems.

It is important to note that while we did reference technology in the typologies defined above, spaces are typically not intended to be defined by a specific equipment list. More commonly, spaces that are created to support making are defined by the type of making that is happening within, for example, additive versus subtractive making or clean spaces versus dirty spaces or initial discovery techniques versus advanced fabrication. Continuing with the references to poultry, think of making as a debate over which came first, the chicken or the egg. A great idea may be inspired by the

Featured Makerspace: West Virginia University's TLC Sandbox

Described as "a research and development space for faculty, graduate students, and staff to assess and test emerging learning technologies" (West Virginia University, n.d.), the Teaching and Learning Commons Sandbox (see Figure 2.7) offers a wide range of technologies and spaces in which to test them. From furniture to green screen rooms, the TLC Sandbox challenges us to think about the many ways in which to interpret the concept of making, pushing beyond fabrication of physical objects to embrace the virtual.

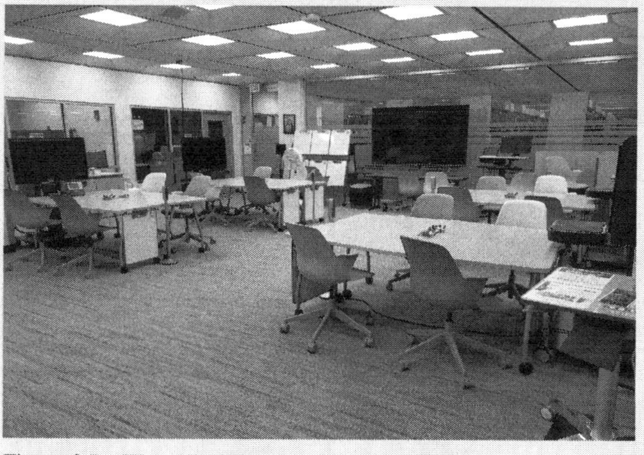

Figure 2.7 West Virginia University's TLC Sandbox.

potential of technology or technology simply makes it possible to manifest that great idea in physical form. Ultimately, makerspaces do tend to share a common equipment list and technology resources, but the beauty of making is derived from the diversity of ideas and the individuals who initiate them. While one makerspace may find the sewing machine to be a little-used technology, another makerspace may see it as central to the makerspace functions.

THE ECOSYSTEM OF MAKING

To further the exploration of making and expanding on the vocabulary of making, the idea of an ecosystem of making is a helpful conceptualization. An ecosystem of making often exists at an institution and includes a range of related spaces that have collectively evolved to support making and the various stages of making from ideation through fabrication and display. It is helpful to understand these related spaces as part of an infrastructure that exists to support broader goals of innovation and entrepreneurship. Making and spaces for making often may seem to exist as independent or focused initiatives, but, more often, they are part of a broader and often less obvious innovation strategy. To encourage collaboration, creative thinking and problem solving, and ideation, institutions are increasingly tapping into makerspaces and the network of related spaces to support students in entrepreneurial endeavors such as starting businesses. While once organic in nature, the contemporary desire to promote entrepreneurship on campus has resulted in formal support and promotion of making in both curricular and cocurricular activities. This support is often manifested in an ecosystem of making. While these associated spaces may or may not be part of what you are planning for your library, it is helpful to be aware of this potential and the ideas that are driving them. Likewise, these associated spaces often become part of activities we will introduce and explore in the second half of the book specific to programming, advocacy, and assessment.

Lounge

While some adhere to the idea of getting right to work, others get more done when they have the opportunity to ease into the task at hand. Just as some workers in the office environment need quiet, heads-down time, others can only function if they have music playing or a movie streaming in the background. A lounge as part of the making ecosystem is highly desirable and is often one of the first spaces where new partnerships are formed. Lounge spaces also serve as a precursor to more formal spaces. Lounges psychologically invite individuals into a makerspace and provide a relaxing atmosphere, to converse casually, and to ease into more direct discussions. Just as the academic library often serves as neutral territory on campus, a place where someone coming from any discipline feels welcome, a lounge serves this same purpose as a precursor to making. This is especially true for individuals new to the process of making or to a makerspace and the equipment and technology often found within.

The creation of this environment might include inviting colors and materials, comfortable furniture, a variety of lighting options, an audiovisual system, among others. Additionally, the ability to define space by reconfiguring it is often highly desirable. Collectively, the environment for the lounge is focused on setting the mood for creativity and creating a variety of lounging options to satisfy the needs of diverse users of the space.

For some, ideas come more freely when they are in spaces unencumbered by tools, equipment, and processes. The lounge offers this. For others, hearing the words *lounge* and *tinkerspace* are cringeworthy as a suggestion that nothing serious is happening. The lounge as a component of a broadly defined makerspace is important in that it allows for the freedom of choice by a diverse population that is makers. Each maker is guided by their own set of principles and work ethic.

Hatchery or Ideation Space

Quite literally, a *hatchery* (sometimes called simply an ideation space) suggests a space where ideas are hatched or born. Such spaces might exist in conjunction with makerspaces, parallel to them, or as part of the actual making space. *Ideation* is the process of generating and pitching ideas through sketching or diagramming. In a hatchery, individuals are provided with a range of tools or supplies to ideate. Markers and markerboards, oversized notepads, and post-it notes are just some examples of what might be seen in a hatchery. Depending on the audience, a range of furniture might be seen, from more formal settings of tables and chairs to beanbag chairs and ottomans. The tools, supplies, and furniture are intended to support the activity of ideation, and ways doing so vary as much as the personality of the innovators. A hatchery is often an enclosed space or a space with some degree of privacy. As ideas are hatched, excitement builds. As a result, these areas can be seen as loud or boisterous as entrepreneurs are passionately talking about their ideas. Likewise, as ideas are hatched, entrepreneurs often desire some degree of privacy to protect their intellectual property.

A hatchery is more about the idea and less about the physical outcomes, which is the focus of a makerspace. When a hatchery exists in conjunction with a makerspace, the intent is to move the idea or process into testing quickly and easily. Entrepreneurs may find themselves moving back and forth between ideation and making as the testing evolves the idea.

Collaboration Space

In some settings, the term *collaboration space* is used. A collaboration space can indicate a range of activities depending on the entrepreneurial setting. In essence, it means just as the name implies, a space where individuals are able to collaborate. What this means can vary greatly, though. For some, a collaboration space might be a pseudonym for a hatchery. The two terms may in fact be describing the same activity. More often, though, a collaboration space often suggests a more formal setting separate from the potentially boisterous hatchery. In this case, entrepreneurs or makers may be collaborating with a faculty member leading a class assignment, or they may be meeting with their project sponsors. The hatchery is seen as the active ideation space, while the collaboration space is a more formal, businesslike setting and often separate from the potential disarray of a space strewn with post-it notes. In this scenario, think of conference tables and chairs arranged for such meetings.

Incubator

Incubators are spaces where ideas are nurtured and formalized. Often separate from other spaces introduced above and perhaps from the initial forms of making, the incubator is the location where ideas move closer to realized outcomes. Ideas will graduate from initial iterations to formalized plans. Such a space might provide access to higher-level making or formalized models and associated testing of ideas and processes. In the incubator, an idea becomes a realized endeavor.

Accelerator

The *accelerator* is, in many ways, the final step of the entrepreneurial journey. An accelerator acts as the next step after incubation, where entrepreneurs are supported in many different ways, depending on need. The goal is to take the idea that has been incubating and formally launch an independent business from that idea. An accelerator may provide a range of spaces and services for a fledgling start-up from office space and a business address to production spaces and packaging and shipping capabilities. The accelerator strives to make the transition from idea to small, start-up business possible, recognizing that capital assets required to start a business are often the roadblock preventing the start-up from happening.

It is important to reiterate that we discuss these related spaces as an overview. As with the various types of makerspaces, the terminology of these related spaces is often freely interpreted and used generically.

Recognizing formalized definitions helps to contextualize the broader ecosystem of making and will assist you in planning your makerspace and envisioning how it might be positioned at your institution. It is beneficial to see making as just one piece of the overall ecosystem; and while the library is likely not intended or prepared to address all making-related needs, it is good to recognize that other resources do often exist. From a library-based makerspace, for example, makers might be referred to other resources for more advanced making or to tap into collaborative opportunities with other makers on campus. Conversely, if this broader ecosystem of making does not exist on your campus, a successful library-based makerspace may ignite interest in creating such a network.

ORGANIZATION OF MAKING

Building on the idea of an ecosystem, it is helpful to recognize that there are several ways to organize the diverse spaces that make up an ecosystem of making. Different and competing factors at an institution can affect this organization. Most obvious, perhaps, is funding. If, as described earlier, entrepreneurship is a goal of an institution, funding may be centralized and originate from the provost and may be intended to support a very specific strategy for creating an ecosystem. If, on the other hand, making is not part of an institution-wide strategy but rather is grounded in individual academic disciplines, there may be no formal or recognizable organization. Yet another model may be even more grassroots, one in which an individual staff member, faculty member, or student has become a sort of entrepreneur on the making frontier. In this case, making may be limited to a single piece of privately owned equipment. Regardless of which reality is playing out at your institution, we offer the following organizational models for your consideration. Such an overview may be helpful for those beginning the planning process for a makerspace or for those pondering how they might evolve making that is already taking place into something more formal.

Centralized vs. Decentralized

A popular juxtaposition related to makerspaces is the idea of centralized versus decentralized organization. Centralized models suggest that making is concentrated in one area or place. This could manifest as a room dedicated to making, a floor dedicated to making, or an entire building with different floors and rooms dedicated to different forms of making. For some institutions, planning this type of organization suggests that some parts of campus are more making centric while others are not focused on making. Regardless of how a centralized model is envisioned, the idea is that makers can feasibly find all or most resources for making in one place or area. Conversely, a decentralized model of making suggests that making happens everywhere or away from a central, concentrated area. The latter is quite common on campuses. For example, 3D printers may be located in residence halls for ease and convenience of student access. Subtractive forms of making such as routers and milling machines might be located in a woodshop, often referred to as *dirty rooms* or *dirty spaces*, while additive forms of making might be located elsewhere on campus and commonly known as *clean rooms* or *clean spaces*. Making is often separated by discipline, type of making, or type of resources provided. Thinking about this model of organization, it is important to consider the advantages and disadvantages of each. Centralized making allows for all resources to be centrally located, making it easy for makers to find what they want. This may, in turn, physically separate the discipline from the making in terms of faculty or staff, their offices and classrooms, and the centralized makerspace. Conversely, the decentralized model suggests that the maker may have to travel between spaces to access the tools they desire for a given process. Centralized versus decentralized is not a matter of right or wrong but rather illustrates the need for careful consideration of the culture on campus and how a given organization of making spaces will either support or hinder making.

Hub and Spoke

The *hub-and-spoke* concept is a form of decentralized organization and may be of special interest to those planning making spaces in a library. In the hub-and-spoke model, the hub is at the center of making. It is the first destination for makers, especially those new to making. At the hub, makers might engage in some preliminary or introductory making but, more often, are using the space in the hub to collaborate and talk through their ideas. When an idea for making surfaces, staff at the hub might then direct makers to other making resources on campus. Think of the hub as a sort of clearinghouse for making, with traffic controllers directing makers to various potential landing sites for actual making.

In the hub-and-spoke model, the spokes are individual makerspaces that exist as offshoots of the hub. Each spoke may have specialized tools or equipment for unique modes of making. Likewise, different spoke locations may be staffed with individuals who are able to assist different levels of making expertise. In a hub-and-spoke model, the organization of making and makers is typically intended to reduce duplication. Rather than every makerspace on campus having the same equipment, you would travel to different locations to access different resources. This reduction in duplication may also allow for a greater range of tools, equipment, and space resources. For example, rather than the same 3D printer at three different locations, each of the three locations may have a different type of 3D printer or printers that are able to print at different qualities. This approach is highly desirable as the expertise of making rises across the maker community.

Mobile

The idea of *mobile makerspaces* or *mobile making* is a popular model when resources are limited or shared. Mobile makerspaces might suggest that resources are available on carts or are otherwise transportable. This approach is common when faculty want to bring making to the classroom rather than taking a class to a makerspace. Tools and equipment are checked out of a central supply and utilized remotely. When considering this form of making, it is important to recognize that not all tools and equipment will be mobile. Some making equipment requires being level for accurate execution. Others require dust and debris collection or exhaust as part of the making process. Still others are simply too large, as in milling and routing machines, to easily be mobile. Generally, the more sophisticated and expensive the equipment, the less likely it will be that those pieces should be mobile.

Another form of mobile making embraces a very different approach, one of simplicity. This form of making might involve a basic collection of portable tools and supplies and a set of instructions for a very specific maker project. These projects are often introductory in nature, intended to expose new makers to a specific set of skills or learning and to entice them into more sophisticated making. This form of mobile making is founded on access and affordability. It is intended to be accessible to those with basic making skills and is often easily scalable in terms of how many individuals can engage in the fun and learning of making at one time.

Virtual Making and Makerspaces

Virtual makerspaces are perhaps the newest of the making scenarios. When individuals speak of virtual making or makerspaces, it typically means one of three things: virtual collaboration, virtual making, or making through virtual reality or augmented reality. Virtual collaboration means that individuals do not have to be in the same physical space to collaborate. Virtual collaboration has evolved quickly from traditional methods of collaboration by telephone, e-mail, and earlier digital tools like Google Docs and Google Sheets to the increasingly popular Microsoft Teams, Slack, and other collaboration-based software. Likewise, the evolution of virtual meeting tools and telepresence technology including Skype, Zoom, GoTo Meeting, and others have all enhanced the capabilities of virtual collaboration and greatly reduced the need for physical, face-to-face meetings and the associated cost of travel.

Virtual making suggests that the act of making can be independent of the actual output. For example, print shops have sprung up in response to new technologies such as 3D printers. Not everyone is able to afford a 3D printer or may not have ready access to the type of printing desired. In the case of virtual making, the maker can generate the digital model and forward the file of that model to a remote printing resource. The remote printer imports the print file and prints the physical model. That model is then mailed to the maker. As 3D printing and other forms of making increase in popularity, this model of making has also become increasingly popular. It allows for speed and efficiency but also opens up opportunities for crowdsourcing and funding of less common or less frequently used equipment by a broader audience, making the affordability of such equipment more likely.

Making through virtual reality suggests that there is never a physical outcome, that all making is experienced virtually or through some digital interface. Across the creative disciplines, this is becoming increasingly popular for both economic reasons and to address the desire for sustainability. Where designers might have once printed out reams of paper to present a project idea, they can now model for the client a three-dimensional walk-thru of the same space. Advances in virtual reality and augmented reality interface have become increasingly realistic and authentic in how users perceive and interact with space and, as a result, these technologies are increasingly helpful to clients in understanding a project direction.

PEOPLE IN MAKERSPACES

It is common to see that those working in a makerspace, especially in a library setting, come from diverse backgrounds. Individuals who staff, manage, and oversee a makerspace may bring specialized knowledge on specific forms of making, may be experts using specific pieces of equipment, or may act as a resource to help patrons of a makerspace understand how best to achieve their making desires. Likewise, the diversity of patrons should be recognized. For example, in the computer project scenario suggested earlier, the hackers might include a computer scientist, an engineer, a product designer, a computer hobbyist, and a host of others with diverse knowledge but a shared interest in and goal of making a computer. Their motivation for engaging with a group of computer hackers may vary greatly. One maker may be partnering with other makers simply to get a computer out of the hack. Others may simply be interested in the challenge of "can we do it?" Another maker may have a vested interest in a new design for user interface but no real need for a computer beyond testing that idea. This diversity of people in makerspaces helps us to understand why no two makerspaces are alike.

While Bagley's definition of makerspaces suggests collaboration as motivation for makerspace patronage, it is also important to recognize independent making. Individuals may tap into the resources and opportunities of a makerspace just as groups of makers do. In their research and reporting on learning environments, Steelcase Inc. suggested that it was important to recognize the diversity of needs of groups and individuals and to provide places that honor this reality, what Steelcase calls "a palette of place" (2014, pp. 8–9). Learning spaces, such as makerspaces, must respond to a continuum of intersecting needs from public to private making and from making alone to making together in groups. Some making happens in private by individuals, while other making happens in public by groups. Likewise, some making happens in private by groups and in public by individuals. The idea of palette of place taps into the psychology of individuals as well as the sociology of education and the sociology of work. As making evolves, individuals' needs and the realities of making may change, resulting in makers being situated at different points along the continuums of public, private, and alone together at different stages of the process.

While modes of making can be divided into discrete categories and be given descriptive titles, making is founded on less rigid rules of organization and order. Making is centered on people and collaborations as much as equipment and spaces. Interest in different equipment ebbs and flows, and it is not uncommon to find a warehouse of unused equipment simply waiting to be utilized on the next big make project. Makers are great at sharing and engage in a sort of swap meet approach to trading one piece of underutilized equipment or technology for another. This sort of free-flowing exchange may ultimately shift the type of making that happens within a given space from one day to the next. Strive to embrace this reality, and you will find the final outcome both more enjoyable and more satisfying.

The physical space and the resources and equipment provided attract makers to a given makerspace. It is important to recognize, though, that individuals often choose to make in specific spaces based not only on these tangible realities but also because of the experiences they have in different makerspaces. These experiences are largely informed by the people who both staff and make in these spaces. Informed by design thinking, be sure to keep empathy at the forefront of the planning process and recognize the role of people in the planning equation.

CONCLUSION

In this chapter, we have offered an overview of design thinking as an approach to use in planning a makerspace. Through the application of this strategy, planning becomes a clear and thoughtful process. Design thinking challenges you to develop an understanding of needs and wants, it asks you to define goals and objects, and ultimately you have the ability to imagine what a potential makerspace might be. The process is both iterative and circular to ensure that many possibilities are explored and that the ultimate outcome is a tried and tested solution.

Also in this chapter, we have described a range of making spaces for your consideration. We have explored the concept of an ecosystem of making as well as offered different organizational strategies for that ecosystem. All of this was intended to help you imagine the possibilities as you progress through the design thinking process.

We concluded the chapter with a reminder that people are at the center of makerspaces. While we recognize that makerspaces are often the result of excitement generated by the latest technology or tool, making has existed and evolved as humans have. Owning this reality will help to ensure that your makerspace continues to remain relevant into the future.

ADDITIONAL READINGS

Anderson, C. (2012). *Makers: The new industrial revolution.* New York, NY: Crown Business.

Burke, J.J. & Kroski, E. (2018). *Makerspace: A practical guide for librarians.* (2nd ed.). Lanham, MD: Rowman & Littlefield.

Hamilton, M. & Schmidt, D.H. (2015). *Make it here: Inciting creativity and innovation in your library.* Santa Barbara, CA: Libraries Unlimited.

REFERENCES

American University. (n.d.). *Makerspace.* Retrieved from https://subjectguides.library.american.edu/c.php?g=833062&p=5948226

Bagley, C.A. (2013, Jan 7). What is a makerspace? Creativity in the library. *ALA TechSource.* Retrieved from http://www.ala.org/tools/article/ala-techsource/what-makerspace-creativity-library

Carnegie Mellon University. (n.d.). *IDeATe.* Retrieved from https://ideate.cmu.edu/facilities/index.html

Curedale, R. (2013). *Design thinking: Process and methods manual.* Topanga, CA: Design Community College Inc.

Parliament. (n.d.). Churchill and the commons chamber. Retrieved from https://www.parliament.uk/about/living-heritage/building/palace/architecture/palacestructure/churchill/

Steelcase Inc. (2014). Active learning spaces. Retrieved from https://www.steelcase.com/content/uploads/2015/01/Steelcase-Education-Insights-Guide-Version-4.pdf

The University of Sydney. (n.d.). *ThinkSpace.* Retrieved from https://library.sydney.edu.au/libraries/thinkspace.html

University of Washington, Tacoma. (n.d.). *3D printing in the library.* Retrieved from https://www.tacoma.uw.edu/learning-research-commons/3d-printing-larc

West Virginia University. (n.d.). *TLC Sandbox.* Retrieved from https://tlcommons.wvu.edu/sandbox

THREE

Planning and Design Considerations for Making and Makerspaces

In this chapter, we will transition into pragmatic considerations of planning and design. Regardless of the size of your envisioned makerspace, you will likely need to involve other individuals and offices at your institution as part of the planning process. In fact, there may be someone on your campus who will assist you in managing the planning process or who might end up taking the lead on formal planning. Likewise, once the space has been planned, you will need to consider how it will be managed and who will oversee it. In the sections that follow, we offer both big-picture considerations and specifics about the physical characteristics and assets to be considered, the people involved in the planning and design process, and the opportunities related to staffing, management, and oversight of your makerspace.

PLANNING AND DESIGN

In the planning and design of a makerspace, you will need to consider a range of space-related realities beginning with the allocation of square footage and the physical location of the proposed makerspace. The physical location and size of the space will serve as the foundation for planning for things like access, safety and security, and considerations for acoustics and climate control of the space. Additionally, the physical location of the makerspace will ultimately be part of what determines the type of equipment that can be used in the space due to code requirements. Beyond this, the planning and design of the space also entails the selection of finishes, materials, and furniture. In this first section of Chapter 3, we offer a number of critical evaluations to undertake as part of the selection process.

Space Allocation

As the planning process for a makerspace begins, determining how much physical space to allocate to a makerspace will likely be one of the first decisions to be made. While some institutions have the resources to add square footage to their physical footprint, more commonly, the square footage for a makerspace is simply carved out of the existing building footprint. Ideally, there will be an opportunity to determine how much space is needed based on programming desires and needs and using a design thinking approach as discussed in Chapter 2. Other times, though, a given amount of space will simply be allocated toward the creation of a makerspace. In the latter instance, the amount of space will certainly dictate what is possible. In recent years, the process of space allocation has become somewhat easier. As libraries move to digital resources, square footage in the building footprint is freed up for other uses. This move to digital resources has gone hand in hand with libraries reimagining how their space is used and the purpose of libraries in the 21st century. Because of this, makerspaces have become increasingly popular additions to the portfolio of libraries as they redefine their purpose and space utilization.

Location

In addition to how much space to allocate to a makerspace, the planning should take into account where in the library the makerspace is to be located. The thoughtful organization of resources within the library is not a new concept in library planning. Library staff have, for decades, thought strategically about how to locate resources based on visibility, traffic flow, and general desires to reach intended audiences through both accidental and intentional collisions with resources. For example, if the makerspace has become a major initiative, it may be important to locate it such that the space has high visibility to library patrons. Visibility is a key marketing strategy in driving makerspace usage and activity. At the same time, making can be either spurred on or stifled by notions of visibility. While it is often desirable to showcase making to generate excitement and attempt to drive others toward making, some makers find that being on display is not desirable and discourages creativity. Space allocation and the physical location of a makerspace should take into account how such decisions might affect makers within.

If there is little to no flexibility in where the proposed makerspace will be located, the planning process should take this into account. Square footage will dictate what types of activities can be included. Additionally, the physical location of the makerspace will determine if things like after-the-fact ventilation are possible. As you begin to evaluate possible uses of an existing space, carefully consider how location provides opportunities for and also limits the kinds of activities that take place within it.

Visual Communication and Wayfinding

How individuals access and use a makerspace depends largely on wayfinding. To appreciate the need for wayfinding, begin by asking yourself how individuals find the makerspace and then how they come to understand what is located within it. A patron's ability to find the space and then take the next step of actually entering it is a major consideration when planning a makerspace in the context of a library. The more immediate wayfinding that happens within the boundaries of the library proper are explored here as part of the planning and design of the makerspace.

Consider the physical relationship between the library and the proposed makerspace. If the desire is to present the makerspace as an extension of the existing library, you will need to visually convey this through the careful selection of interior finishes and materials including things like flooring materials, wall and ceiling treatment, furniture, and lighting. Also consider the continuity of signage and other graphic elements. It is important to note that the eye and therefore the subconscious mind pick up on subtle changes in wayfinding strategy. If your intent is continuity, focus on all parts of the visual communication and branding of the space: color, fonts, and types of graphics used so that the new makerspace visually flows out of the existing library space.

Conversely, the desire may be to present the makerspace as a new or separate addition to the library. In this case, use the same considerations above but strive for obvious contrast to suggest distinctions. For example, if the library proper utilizes dim, soft lighting, the new makerspace might be designed in contrast to this with bright, crisp lighting. From a distance, the space will be illuminated and psychologically attract patrons to investigate the new and the unknown. Wall paint and other interior finishes have a similar affect. If the library proper utilizes warm wood tones and a neutral color palette, the makerspace might be designed to leverage glass and metal with rich, saturated hues. Either way, consideration must be given specifically to how the makerspace will align or not with the existing visuals based on what impression you want the makerspace to make on the patron.

Access and Security

Making and the associated creative processes are not always neatly or conveniently undertaken during normal hours of operation. The desire for making may occur late at night or may extend overnight. As the location of a potential makerspace is being evaluated, consideration should be given to access to the space and how the makerspace and the tools and equipment found within will be secured. As a new driver of activity, the location of the makerspace may be most conveniently located near entry points to the library facility for ease of access control and to allow for the potential of unique hours of operation between disparate areas of the library. Many libraries have extended or overnight hours for specific floors; this may be a desirable consideration to ensure easy and convenient access by patrons. At the same time, the makerspace may contain easily portable tools, supplies, expensive equipment, and potentially hazardous processes. For this reason, security and the ability to monitor the space and/or those entering and exiting it will be desirable. Be sure to check with your institutional policies specific to monitoring techniques to understand what is allowed. Some institutions have implemented monitoring protocols, while others limit the types of monitoring that are allowed. This can include guidelines on how and where monitoring can take place.

Acoustics

In conjunction with location, one key factor to consider when siting the makerspace within the library is acoustics. While libraries have moved away from the tradition of primarily quiet space and discouraging conversation in favor of silence, makerspaces, by nature, are not quiet spaces.

Making is a collaborative process, and with the potential to be equipment intensive, the result can be a space that generates a good deal of noise, both permitted and unwanted. Thinking of location and the implication of noise generated in the space, consider adjacencies or the spaces that will exist in proximity to the makerspace. Such concerns will be driven by the makerspace program, but, generally, it will be undesirable to locate a makerspace next to quiet study spaces. And, depending on the types of equipment to be utilized in the space and building construction, it may be important to avoid locating a makerspace above or below quiet space. For these reasons it is not uncommon to find makerspaces located in the lower levels of the library. In some cases, there is a possibility to reimagine broad swaths of space and to reorganize where various areas and department are located within the building to accommodate a makerspace program. But if not, be sure to take the space above into consideration and be proactive in heading off noise complaints and expectations for noise levels within the makerspace proper.

Visual Access

A common desire when planning a makerspace is to put making on display. The thought process here is that by putting making on display, it will attract others to the space who are curious about making. This type of display is a form of built-in marketing for the space, revealing to outsiders the potential of the space and what tools and equipment are available within it. Projects that are displayed might inspire creativity in others.

At the same time, spaces should be designed with an awareness of the diversity of potential makers in mind. Not all makers want to be on display. They may be shy about their skill level with making, with the types of making they are engaging in, or desire to keep their outcomes private until they are ready for sharing. For example, if the makerspace is intended to break down gender stereotypes and empower makers, male makers assuming that "sewing is for girls" may be shy about sitting at a sewing machine, or individuals who have never been exposed to handheld power tools may not feel comfortable developing dexterity with them while being watched. Likewise, making is also an evolutionary process. Makers may be experimenting with techniques and not want to be judged by those early outcomes. Additionally, it may be desired that the products of making be kept secret until a formal presentation or exhibition takes place, thus making privacy a key planning determinant. Consideration should be given to all of these during the planning process. While the makerspace may not be able to accommodate every need or desire, the plan of the space will ideally allow individuals some flexibility in how and where they make within the space.

Heating, Ventilation, and Air-Conditioning (HVAC)

Yet another consideration related to location will be the impact of the makerspace on HVAC needs and requirements, more specifically ventilation and air-conditioning. Making and the related processes and equipment can greatly affect the air quality. 3D printers, for example, depending on the type of printing being undertaken, may release fumes into the air that require specific venting to the exterior of the building. Similarly, many subtractive processes of making (milling, routing, carving) often generate and/or release particulates into the interior environment. These particulates may need to be either vented or collected and removed from the space for health and safety reasons. Likewise, equipment involved in making often generates heat. Because of this and the potential for a general increase in the number of patrons per square foot of space may require that the air-conditioning of the makerspace environment be specifically redesigned to ensure both safety and comfort.

It is important to note that it is helpful to be aware of many of the above considerations as you embark on the planning of a makerspace. Each can be useful when evaluating the feasibility of possible locations for a new makerspace. That said, you will need to consult with the appropriate offices and professionals introduced earlier in this chapter in determining if all requirements have been met, as these factors are mandated by law and regulated by code to ensure the health, safety, and well-being of both the occupants of the makerspace and the broader library patron population.

Furniture, Finishes, and Equipment

Whether part of the process of establishing the physical size of the space or a result of a simple space allocation, the furniture, finishes, and equipment selected will certainly play into the success or failure of a makerspace. As above, some of these decisions are regulated by code and are thus offered here to promote fruitful conversations during the planning process. Other decisions, those specific to furniture, interior finishes, and equipment for the space, are not regulated or not to the same extent. Even so, an awareness of how these components of the interior design can impact both the space and the users of the space will surely improve the decision-making process.

Materials and Finishes

Surface materials and finishes set the tone for the interior. As part of our perceptions of the space, the visuals are part of what draws users into a space and can create a sense of welcome. Beyond the visual perceptions, though, consider how surface materials can be cleaned and otherwise cared for and repaired, and how they perform against certain kinds of stain-causing agents. The materials and finishes chosen for a space contribute to its longevity and implicate care and maintenance of the space. In the three sections below, we overview three primary considerations of the interior: vertical surfaces, horizontal surfaces, and flooring.

Countertops and Work Surfaces (Horizontal Surfaces)

When considering and evaluating materials for countertops and work surfaces, think about hand tools being dropped on or slid across a countertop. Scuffing, scratching, and denting can quickly deteriorate the visuals of a space yet may not impact performance. Consider, for example, the effect of heat production by equipment and heat-producing tools, everything from hot glue guns, soldering irons, and ironing machines to stationary equipment that may need to sit on a countertop versus being freestanding.

Surfaces are available in a range of materials such as laminate or laminate-like products that are durable and easy to clean while also resisting many types of stain-causing spills and accidents. Wood, while also durable, is not as resistant to damage as laminates. Here, though, the difference is that wood can more easily be repaired and can be brought back to life in many cases more readily than laminate surfaces. Likewise, wood is often viewed as adding visual appeal to a space. It is not uncommon to hear designers and patrons alike describe an interior that incorporates wood as "warm and inviting," for example. Stone or man-made solid surface materials such as Corian may be desirable for their durability and repairability but will typically cost more than their laminate or wood counterparts. Likewise, metal and metal-wrapped surfaces can be highly desirable for durability and stain resistance but should be evaluated in terms of the visual implications for a space. If using metal surfaces, a space can quickly take on an industrial or laboratory-like visual quality. Porous surfaces such as a cement countertop are often highly desirable for their versatility and visual design quality but are often more susceptible to staining and damage resulting from dropped equipment. In collaborative spaces, in particular, versus production spaces, work surfaces may also be available from some manufacturers in a porcelain or marker surface or come with the ability to install pads of sketching paper right on the surface to support ideation and collaborative ideation.

Regardless of the surface material, be sure to also consider the edge of the surface and the edge material. Edges sustain their own types of wear and potential damage, susceptible to things bumping into them or knocking against them such as carts or tools and equipment being pulled across them when being moved on and off of the surface. Likewise, this is a primary interface for the user, where the user's arm rests when working at a counter. If long-term activity is expected at one location, a softer material and/or a rolled versus sharp edge may be more desirable.

Walls (Vertical Surfaces)

The walls of the makerspace should not be viewed simply as space dividers. While dividing space is important along with the acoustic properties that come with it, walls and vertical surfaces also present opportunities for visual communication and can be used to address unique functional needs as well.

Paint or some type of paper or vinyl wallcovering have long been part of the standard treatment of walls, the thinking being that color or visual patterns and textures enhance the interior design. At the same time, just as with horizontal surfaces discussed above, potential damage and long-term durability should be considered. For example, impact damage to a painted wall can easily be repaired at very little cost. Likewise, changes to the design strategy can easily be undertaken for painted surfaces as needs and desires for the interior changes. Paper and vinyl wallcoverings, on the other hand, are seen as a step up in terms of durable wall treatments but are not as easily changed and often cost more to do so.

There are other possibilities when thinking about and planning for vertical surfaces. In many cases, walls can be considered a projection surface, eliminating the need for separate projection surfaces and screens. Likewise, moving beyond the potential of markerboards, the wall as a writing surface has become increasingly popular. This can be accomplished by coating the wall with chalkboard paint or applying a wallcovering that turns the wall plane into a writing surface that can be wiped clean and reused continuously. If exploring this potential, be sure to investigate the required writing tools and products needed to clean the surface, and make those available as part of provided supplies for the space and account for them in the budget to avoid irreparable damage. Once accustomed to writing on wall surfaces, if the appropriate writing tools and cleaning agents are not available, users will default to what they have available, and not all marks can be removed. It is helpful to make signage alerting users of the space of guidelines for use in order to maintain the long-term aesthetics of the space.

Another possibility for a vertical surface is to use the face of walls as pinup space. Rather than hard surfaces, consider creating a tackable surface where makers can pin up sketches, photographs, and other visuals displays. There are numerous ways to accomplish this, from simply applying a material such as cork or homasote to an existing wall or, alternatively, reimagining how the wall itself is constructed. A relatively inexpensive tackable surface can be created by wrapping rigid foam with a textile and providing t-pins for pinup display. Likewise, another creative strategy is to embed a magnetic surface into the wall design or apply it to the wall plane after the fact and use magnets rather than pins for display purposes.

The different approaches will impact both the long-term performance of the space and its functionality but also the budget. Consider the options carefully and match the various design strategies to the desired outcomes of the space.

Flooring and Floor Materials

The design strategy for the floor is critical. Choosing to apply a flooring material or simply polishing a concrete floor, for example, can have long-term implications for the space as well as how it will look and how it will perform over time. Function of the space must be considered. For example, while carpet might be desired for its acoustic qualities and comfort for the maker, it can also be a headache for custodial staff. If, for example, you have making that involves textiles and straight pins, both tend to end up on the floor. Pins, in particular, can be dangerous when they become lodged in carpet and can damage cleaning equipment. Conversely, if the space involves liquids as part of the making processes or if food and beverages are allowed in the space, carpet or hard-surface materials such as stone or tile may not be desirable compared to laminate or vinyl materials. The latter tend to be more easily cleaned and lack the porous quality that results in liquids being absorbed into floor coverings and remaining as a permanent stain.

At the same time, when considering flooring materials and options, both acoustics and comfort should be taken into account. Soft and porous materials tend to absorb noise more readily, helping to make the space quieter and generally improving the overall acoustics. Likewise, soft flooring materials create a cushion underfoot, which make long-term standing at work counters more comfortable for makers. The strategy for flooring can be variable, with different materials used in different areas specific to need and functional appropriateness. Likewise, area rugs can be considered part of the overall strategy to soften areas with lots of hard surface.

Furniture

One of the greatest expenses of a design is the furniture. Several key considerations should be made when evaluating furniture for a makerspace. For example, if the intent of the makerspace is to encourage collaboration, furniture that is mobile and able to be reconfigured and rearranged by makers is key. As makers begin to work together, they may wish to push tables together to make collaboration easier or more effective specific to how their team functions. Likewise, furniture may be reconfigured to facilitate a specific process. Arranging tables in a long run in a sort of factory-line scenario is an example of an alternative arrangement that is commonly found in makerspaces. Both examples illustrate how makers might want to rearrange furniture to suit their specific needs or a specific making process, and show the importance of specifying furniture that allows for such reconfiguration possibilities.

Along with rearranging furniture, furniture that is adjustable in an array of scenarios is highly desirable and useful to makers. From height adjustments to furniture that expands or contracts in different directions can allow for more productive making spaces. Long spans of making and the inability to move between sitting and standing can be unhealthy. By offering furniture that is adjustable, makers can create in spaces that are ergonomically correct but may also contribute to long-term health and a sense of well-being. Likewise, such adjustments can contribute to goals of accessibility and meeting Americans with Disabilities Act (ADA) requirements.

As furniture is evaluated for a makerspace, keep ideas of performance and durability at the forefront of consideration. For example, seating that is easy to clean yet comfortable is key. Food that is stuck in crevices, sticky spills on work surfaces, and stains all contribute to how the space is perceived and, in turn, when and if someone chooses to utilize the space. As mentioned earlier in the chapter, choose from vendors whose products are intended for the type of activities that will take place in the space. Upholstery should be rated for commercial use versus residential use, for example. As such, it is inherently more durable and holds up to different types of cleaning and cleaning products. Additionally, the types of materials specified and the design of the furniture can and do contribute to care and maintenance and ultimately the overall cleanliness and health of the space. Crevices in furniture or the type of material specified to upholster furniture may collect or trap dirt, food, and other contaminants. This in turn may attract pests and ultimately affect the long-term health and use of the space. Color too is an important consideration. Building on the previous discussion, here we might consider color in terms of its ability to hide versus highlight dirt and wear and tear. White finishes notoriously reveal dirt, whereas color and materials with visual patterns and texture help to conceal it.

If you are not in a position to purchase new furniture for your makerspace, embrace the reuse of existing furniture as part of your makerspace's brand. In many ways, this approach might be just as appealing to makers, who may feel more comfortable making in a space that is not shiny and new. A bit of patina may create a psychologically more inviting space for makers, while a space with all-new furniture may feel off-limits to making processes that are potentially messy or dirty. Beyond this, you might also consider having a community of makers create the furniture for the space as part of a make event prior to or in conjunction with the official opening of the space. Nothing gets makers more in touch with a space than inviting them in to be part of its creation. Things like reclaimed doors and sawhorses can quickly be turned into tables for a collaboration space, while crates and pallets can be repurposed for seating and tool storage. Creativity and engagement with makers are the goal in this approach.

Lighting

As noted in earlier discussions, consider the aesthetic appeal of lighting and lighting fixtures while balancing that with function. Lighting is a key component of setting the mood of a space. Dim lighting can be comfortable and inviting, encouraging lowered voices and quieter conversations, while bright light can be offensive and lead to eyestrain. Alternatively, if light levels are too low, it may be hard to see the task at hand or be dangerous if the light is so dim that it prevents visual acuity. Two primary considerations should be taken into account: first, the range of activities and the type of lighting needed for each, and second, the diversity of users in a space. Activities, age, and ability all play into the type and amount of light to be provided in the design of a makerspace. Consider varying the sources of light, both in terms of luminaires (fixtures) and the type of lamps (bulbs). Likewise, consider user control of lighting. Things like how close or far away it is from a work surface or task, being able to focus light in a specific direction, and the ability to control the intensity of lighting will all make for improved safety and functionality. The more patrons of a space are able to control their environment, the more likely they are to use it, use it safely, and be happy with it. By providing diverse lighting options, mobile furniture, and a range of finishes, the resulting design allows makers to self-select into a scenario that best meets their needs and the demands of varied tasks they might be working on.

Ultimately, the design of a space is a balancing act between aesthetics and function. The most durable and easy-to-clean components for an interior can also often be the least visually pleasing and may lack tactile appeal. Conversely, the curves and textures of contemporary interiors may exist counter to goals of cleaning and maintenance. Revert to the design thinking approach when making decisions about the space, and rely on an understanding of the goals and intent for the space and match the interior components to those goals.

PLANNING AND DESIGN PARTNERS

It is often assumed that it would be easier and less expensive if we just "do it ourselves." The reality is that the built-in administrative and operational structures of an institution created to support construction projects are often a reflection of federal, state, or local regulation; concerns for safety and security; and for economic reasons. Partnering with any or all of the following departments or individuals will ideally make your role in the creation of a makerspace easier as well as help protect you, the users of the space, and your budget. Professionals involved at each step of the planning and design process have specialized training and experience that will help to make the process faster and ideally smoother. They will help uncover questions about the project that you might not have thought about.

In-House Personnel

Internal to the library, there may be someone whose job it is to manage library space and how it is used. As a first step, seek out this individual and share your interest in and ideas for a makerspace. This person may be an in-house facilities manager or an interior designer with specialized knowledge on the planning and implementation process for space-related projects. Alternatively, this will be a librarian who has been asked to take ownership of such responsibilities on behalf of the library and oversees space-related projects with a keen eye and consideration for diverse internal considerations as well as an understanding of the broader implications of federal, state, regional, and campus regulation. A good place to start is the dean's office to inquire about who this person might be or where to start the process. You might also consult the staff directory or an internal organizational chart that lists people, their positions, and their responsibilities. If such a position exists in your library, this person will likely have established relationships with many if not all of the people and offices we will describe in the following sections.

Institutional Planning Office

Most colleges and universities have a planning office that is responsible for administering and overseeing the overall space of a campus, how it is used, and by whom. If you are leading the planning process, it will be important to get in touch with this office or the university officials responsible for such matters. Whether you are planning for newly constructed space or converting existing space, the planning office is often the entity on campus that tracks statistical data specific to space use and reports that data to the appropriate state entity. Most states track such data as a requirement of being a publicly funded entity. Likewise, a college or university planning office often administers the capital budget and helps to coordinate funding requests external to the university. A makerspace may or may not be part of a larger educational initiative by your institution, by the state, or by the federal government and thus may qualify for funding or can be plugged into a near- or long-term budget model of financial planning.

Architecture, Design, and Construction Office

Parallel to or in partnership with the planning office, your college or university may also have an office of in-house personnel who design or oversee the design of space. Moving beyond the planning office's role of planning for and allocating space, an architecture, design, and construction office may undertake actual design of space including needs assessment, physical space planning, planning and coordinating mechanical systems, assuring code compliance including accessibility and code compliance, and material selections. This office is often also responsible for ensuring that new projects adhere to university standards specific to graphics, wayfinding, furniture, and all things related to the interior. For example, your institution may have requirements for using specific vendors as part of a campus-wide purchasing agreement program or have partnerships with specific contractors who will carry out specific parts of any given project.

Conversely, depending on the size of your project, the scope of work required, and the project capacity, the architecture, design, and construction office is also responsible for partnering with external resources to undertake the design of new or renovated space on campus that extends beyond the abilities and capacity of the internal team. It is not uncommon for a university to have in-house designers, architects, and engineers who act as project managers for several campus projects at the same time. These individuals will oversee and coordinate with external designers, architects, and engineers who actually create the design, while the in-house personnel ensure compliance with campus standards and act as the point person for the institution and coordinate with the library.

Depending on the scale and scope of your makerspace project, you may find that you will work closely with a facilities department or office on a range of services from moving furniture to discharging physical assets such as furniture and equipment to university surplus. Likewise, services such as the painting, signage, and access control (key, swipe card, touchpad, or other forms of access) are often also housed within a facilities organization. It is important to note that most campuses have a facilities office not simply for convenience but rather for safety and budgetary reasons. Having a trained staff for these types of services helps to prevent injury and helps to ensure that the university standards are adhered to. Your institution may have, for example, an agreement to purchase a specific brand of interior paint. By entering into this purchasing agreement, it saves the institution money, and a facilities painter knows the particulars of brand, type, and colors that should be used in a given situation and both the correct process to acquire the supplies and how those supplies should be utilized and waste disposed of.

Purchasing or Procurement Office

Another office on campus that you will likely work with during the planning and implementation stage of a makerspace project is the purchasing or procurement office. This office can assist you on a range of needs and resources from negotiating and approving various contracts to offering guidance on where and how to purchase everything from furniture and equipment to supplies after the space is up and running. It is important to engage with this office sooner rather than later during the planning process. This office often has existing relationships with vendors and manufacturers that include buying discounts or guidelines for quality to save the institution money and to safeguard it against inferior products and services. Often, if you are working with one of the other offices mentioned earlier, they will already have a relationship with purchasing and/or know what vendors, manufacturers, and service providers have been preapproved to expedite the process. Because makerspaces do often involve unique equipment and supplies, it is helpful to start the conversation about the space early and to recognize that some items or services may require first-time or extended approval processes. Again, if you are partnering with a planning office or an architecture, design, and construction office, they will likely recognize this, but it never hurts to be aware of it and to bring it up in ini tial meetings as makerspaces are unique from other construction projects that have happened on campus.

Your makerspace may or may not be the first one at your institution or even in your library. While this book is intended to serve as a practical planning guide to the process of establishing a makerspace, we also encourage you to reach out to other makerspaces, both at your institution and beyond. This will allow you an opportunity to benchmark your planning process and ultimately fine-tune the mission and vision for your own makerspace.

On your own campus, check to see what resources are already provided and what technology is available. You may or may not want to duplicate those resources, depending on demand. Likewise, as you plan your own space, you can get a sense of how other makerspaces are operated—everything from hours of operation to guidelines for training on equipment. This will be an opportunity to find your place within the existing network of makerspaces but to also distinguish yourself in the field of makerspaces that potential users can choose from.

Perhaps most importantly, reach out to other makerspaces and individuals that oversee and use them. By doing this, you can ask others what they have learned from their process and also observe things you would mirror or do differently. You can get a sense of what users of the space think about a given makerspace and why they choose a given space over another. In our research for the writing of this book, we visited a number of makerspaces. In true maker fashion, we were enthusiastically invited into each space by individuals with oversight responsibilities who shared with us what they offered and how they operated. Likewise, each recounted stories of successes and challenges intended to help others.

STAFFING, MANAGEMENT, AND OVERSIGHT

One early concern often expressed by individuals when embarking on the creation of a makerspace is the question of who will manage or oversee it. The very technology that is often credited with sparking the contemporary maker movement—3D printers, laser cutters, and the like—is also often the thing that creates the greatest sense of anxiety related to managing a makerspace. There are often individuals in the library who are prepared to embrace new technologies, but if you are not one of them, face these fears head-on and consider the following as possible ways to manage and overcome technology-related concerns. In this section, we will offer suggestions and considerations for management and oversight of a makerspace as well as offer thoughts on how to manage anxiety related to this role.

Program Managers

Certainly, if funding allows, hiring a program manager for the makerspace is an option. It is perhaps the easiest and most efficient approach but also may be the least likely to happen in today's budget climate. A program manager can undertake a whole range of responsibilities and duties from planning and setting up the space to bringing technology expertise to the day-to-day operation of the space. Conversely, hiring a program manager may also be the least desirable. Hiring someone from outside the library realm can set the tone that the makerspace is the "other" and not inherently part of the library. Colocating nonlibrary activities in the library has become a popular trend at many institutions for things like academic tutoring and advising. Colocated activities such as these often do not fall under the direct oversight of library administration and, because of this, can result in culture clashes between the disparate groups. With this in mind, if the goal is to create a library makerspace and not simply locate a makerspace inside the walls of the library, plan strategically to integrate the space from the very beginning. Take care to be thoughtful about how new personnel are hired and onboarded so a sense of belonging is established for all involved.

Librarians and Library Staff

If you are reading this book, you are likely one of the best individuals to step up to the plate and manage or develop a strategy for managing the makerspace. You obviously have a vested interest in the topic or you would not be reading this book. Curiosity is perhaps the most important quality a person can have when it comes to makerspaces. Remember, makerspaces were borne out of the DIY movement, and technology will likely be only one aspect of the total offering of your makerspace. As you embark on the planning process, leverage your existing knowledge and skills. Whether it be locating resources, building collections, or some other form of being resourceful, leverage your own strengths and skills. Jump in and learn any one of a number of software packages available to makers, from basic to advanced. Know that there is an abundance of tutorials for equipment and its operation, everything from hard copy instruction manuals that are packaged with equipment to YouTube videos. Because today's maker movement is tied to a DIY philosophy, several self-help resources have been developed to get individuals with every level of experience up and running. A basic 3D printing tutorial, for example, will have you printing in as little as a few hours. From there you can expand your skills and expertise as needed and desired. You may be surprised to find that makers will embrace you as much for your can-do attitude as they will for any expertise you may already have specific to making.

In addition, strive to create community by soliciting others in the library to take part. Avoidance is often the response to fear and anxiety related to technology. By inviting others to take part, you are beginning to break down those fears. Model the belief in and power of collaboration for makerspace users. You will likely be praised for reaching out to others in the search for how to do something, and by doing so, you are both learning how to do something and demonstrating how collaboration actually works. In reality, this is what making is all about. Curiosity leads to exploration, which leads to collaboration. The result is an outcome that can satisfy the initial goal of making something or it can act as a prototype that is critiqued, reimagined, and reiterated toward more closely hitting the targeted outcome goal. If your makerspace population is new to making, this sort of approach is likely exactly what they will expect. Few visitors to the makerspace will expect you to be an expert. They will benefit from you being a guide, though. Conversely, if your audience is more advanced users, they are likely going to be happy to simply have access to resources and will look to librarians and library staff for assistance with scaffolding to support their exploration.

Student Employees

Consider the range of benefits related to employing students. Students who qualify for a federal work-study program can be a valuable resource, and it provides a convenient, on-campus employment opportunity for them. Typically, work-study programs award enough money to employ students for up to ten hours a week. While you will need to be flexible in working with students who are juggling employment with academics, a work-study scenario is mutually beneficial to both the library and the student employee. Work study is often administered through the human resources office, which is a good starting point to learn more about this potential on your specific campus.

Employing students is a wonderful way to support the operation of a makerspace but is also an opportunity to tap into knowledge and skills students may have related to technology and equipment. Especially during the initial days, weeks, or months of operation, it will be helpful to have students who can support other students in using the space. Consider reaching out to departments or programs that might also have makerspaces or that might utilize making as part of their curriculum and offer employment opportunities or cocurricular programs to them and their students. This begins to create an energy in the space that will be important to its ongoing operation. Having supportive staff also helps to alleviate some of the anxiety individuals new to a makerspace may be experiencing.

Likewise, if your library does employ student workers, consider rotating them through the space during their work schedule not only to support the needs of the space but also to expose them to diverse opportunities for learning. Whether they are makers themselves or not, there will always be tasks that need to be completed within the makerspace that the student worker will be able to undertake. This opportunity for students to engage with the space, both formally and informally, will be beneficial by exposing them to making. It will also help you to promote the space through a sort of alternative, informal means of marketing and advertising. Students will talk to other students about things they see and do in the library makerspace, hence spreading the excitement. We discuss programming and marketing as separate topics and in more depth later in the book as well.

Faculty and Staff

Consider partnering with faculty and staff in departments and programs that may have expertise specific to making technology. Offer to host workshops, lunch-and-learns, or after-hours maker events for librarians and library staff as a learning opportunity about making and the related technology. Such events can be informative but also fun and will help alleviate anxiety about the technology, the space, and changes happening within the library. Likewise, this becomes yet another opportunity to engage with faculty toward future collaborations and for them to better understand what resources are available and how the library, librarians, and library staff might be partners on future endeavors.

As you ponder the options for staffing, management, and oversight of your makerspace, think about how you want it to fit within the larger context of the library and the institution as a whole. It may be easier to staff and manage the space using library personnel, but by inviting others into the operational functions of the space, you are broadening your potential audience and user base. You will want to consider how different funding options may influence operation of the space specific to personnel. Finally, be cognizant of the idea that people are part of the branding of a makerspace. From a design thinking perspective, recognize how the people who work in, manage, and oversee the makerspace ultimately act as part of its marketing and advertising.

MAINTENANCE, SAFETY, AND OPERATION

In addition to the physical planning and design of a makerspace, planning for general maintenance, safety, and operation of the space as well as the tools and equipment found within it should also be considered. Three factors contribute to this thinking and planning: the cost of equipment, building codes and regulations, and the general feeling of comfort that makers have working in a makerspace.

Equipment Cost

First, the cost of equipment commonly found in a makerspace can represent a major investment on the part of your organization. Therefore, you will want to be sure that it is maintained in such a way that protects this investment. The lack of or improper maintenance of equipment is the quickest way to deteriorate it or even render it unusable. Procedures should be established per the manufacturer's guidelines specific to maintenance, including cleaning, to ensure the longevity of equipment and the quality of outcomes produced on the various pieces of equipment. These procedures are often compiled in a binder and kept within the space. Complementing the binders, staff responsible for maintenance should be oriented to correct procedures through formalized training. In both instances, each tool or piece of equipment should be addressed with guidelines established for all of the following:

- What cleaning supplies should or should not be used
- Where and how cleaning supplies should be stored and handled
- When and how to clean various parts of an individual piece of equipment
- How and where to dispose of waste as a result of cleaning

To illustrate this point, we might use the example of the sewing machine common to many makerspaces. A maintenance binder would indicate when sewing machines should be oiled, if and how to clean the sewing machine before and after oiling, the type of oil to be used for machine lubrication, where to store the oil for the sewing machine, what parts of the sewing machine should be oiled, how much oil should be used, and what to do in the case of spills or accidental over-oiling. Additionally, there should be a document to record when a machine has been oiled so others know what actions have been taken and when. All of this is intended to keep the sewing machine in good working order but also to ensure that the items being sewn are not damaged either by a poorly operating machine or by the oil used to maintain the machine. A detailed, step-by-step process eliminates questions and helps those managing a makerspace feel comfortable about maintenance they are undertaking or overseeing. Well-maintained machines will attract makers just as poorly maintained machines will deter them.

Building Codes and Regulations

Second, regional, state, and federal regulation likely require that you plan for and establish guidelines to ensure safety as well as a procedure to follow when something goes wrong. Your makerspace—depending on the size of your organization, the type of equipment and materials available for use in the space, and the related processes undertaken to operate the equipment and handle materials—may be governed by workplace safety and health standards as outlined by the Occupational Safety and Health Administration (OSHA). OSHA standards are intended to protect employees in their workplace and establish certain rights for employees to ensure this. OSHA standards address everything from the reporting guidelines of employee illnesses and injuries on up. More information on this topic is available at OSHA's website, www.osha.gov. It is helpful and perhaps reassuring to know that adhering to these federal standards is part of what your design and planning partners, both those on your campus or those you hire externally, will help you with. Additionally, constructed environments are also governed by some sort of fire safety standards to protect occupants, often those of the National Fire Protection Association (NFPA). Similar to OSHA, NFPA sets forth standards of safety but focuses more specifically on fire, electrical, and similar hazards. As with OSHA, your planning partners will help support you in knowing about and meeting the safety standards established by your state or local municipality. Safety guidelines and procedures are most commonly compiled in a binder and housed within the space. Additionally, signage is often used to reinforce guidelines and procedures set forth in binders or to call out high-risk scenarios. It is also common to establish regular safety training, annual risk reviews, and new employee and patron orientations to establish or refresh safety standards.

Comfort

Third, makers who have clear understanding of how to use tools and equipment in a space are more likely to use that space and use it correctly and with comfort. Counter to common belief, rules and guidelines can put makers at ease rather than causing them to feel restricted as they are keenly aware of the dangers of poorly performing equipment and dangerous situations and how these can negatively impact making. As an example, a 3D printer that is not properly leveled can cause a print job to fail, resulting in wasted time and material and ultimately causing frustration on the part of the maker.

Similar to maintenance, the correct operation of equipment is largely governed by the manufacturer. Establishing any additional guidelines for equipment operation can build on what the manufacturer has already outlined. While most all equipment comes with operating instructions, other avenues can be explored. More passive approaches might include posted signage with basic instructions, with more detailed instructions more commonly compiled in a binder. More active approaches to delivering instruction on equipment operation could take the form of classes or workshops, which are especially helpful for new users of the makerspace and new employees. Additionally, the classes and workshops offer more dynamic engagement during which makers have an opportunity to ask questions in ways that passive approaches do not. Active approaches also offer you the chance to build community by gathering makers with a collective interest in the same space at the same time. Regardless of the approach(es) utilized, the guidelines should typically outline safe operation, the type and size of materials that can be used with a given piece of equipment, what a machine is to be used for, and what to do when something goes wrong. Going back to the example of the sewing machine used earlier, an operations binder might include sections on each of the following:

- Where or how to turn machines on and off
- Warnings about moving parts and potential dangers

- The type of materials that can or cannot be sewn on a particular machine (some machines are not built for bulk or durable fabrics, and likewise, some machines are not appropriate for sewing delicate materials)
- A description of various attachments or accessories that might be available for use on a given machine
- A needle diagram to match the sewing needle to the project
- How to properly thread a machine
- How to adjust tension
- How to clear a knot or jam in the machine
- Descriptions and directions for basic functions
- How to change between stitch types and stitch spacing
- A "Frequently Asked Questions" section
- A troubleshooting guide
- Where to find additional parts such as replacement needles, bobbins, and so on.

Some combination of the various approaches is advisable as makers learn in different ways and your making audience will likely appreciate the opportunity to choose how to engage in such activities. Also, while you may offer workshops or classes, it is helpful to also have signage and reference binders to reinforce learning and to provide on-demand answers to common questions and situations that may arise in the makerspace.

It is important to note that the more complicated the equipment or process, the more expensive the equipment; and the higher the risk to the user, the more active the engagement should be specific to safety and operation. It is not uncommon for makerspaces to require formal training on tools and equipment before individuals are granted access to some spaces or allowed to use the resources found within. Some makerspaces segregate equipment and processes that are higher-risk scenarios under lock and key and require that individuals schedule time to use these spaces. This can often require casual or direct supervision as well, depending on the situation. All of this allows managers of a makerspace to verify that safety and operation training has been completed or to deliver it on demand. While the general tenor of a makerspace is to inspire and generate excitement around making, some boundaries must be established to ensure safety and to avoid damage to tools, equipment,

Figure 3.1 3D printer warning signage used at University of Washington, Tacoma.

and spaces. Some damage is easy to fix, but you will want to avoid having to continually repair equipment due to poor operational practices. Not only is this costly, but equipment downtime is also a detriment to making.

To help illustrate the above, we offer two examples of how different makerspaces have addressed maintenance, safety, and operation within their given makerspace. First, Figure 3.1 showcases the signage used at a 3D printer in the Learning and Research Commons at the University of Washington, Tacoma. The signage calls out specific warnings about a hot surface to users who may be unfamiliar with 3D printing. It should also be noted that the 3D printer is located near a service desk so casual oversight of the 3D printer might alert staff to patrons who could benefit from guidance specific to operation and safety. Likewise, formal training has been instituted as a precursor to using the 3D printer.

As a second example, we offer the table of contents from the American University Library's *Makerspace Employee Handbook* (see Figure 3.2). A review of this table of contents reveals that it contains a broad overview of the makerspace as well as specific instructions and guidelines for use of both the equipment and space. The handbook is supplemented with numerous illustrations to provide clear direction to users intended to ensure proper operation and to increase safety. While it takes time to create such a document, the return on this investment will certainly pay for itself both in training time and in preventing potentially costly downtime or equipment replacement as a result of improper use.

Additionally, American University has an online orientation and requires that users sign a waiver prior to using the makerspace.

CONTENTS

Welcome 4
Location, Access, & Support 5
Makerspace Guidelines 6
Workbenches
  3D Creation 7
    3D Printing for Patrons 9
    3D Printing for Staff 11
      Basic Process 11
      Information about the Ultimaker 11
        Changing the filament 13
      Simplify3D 15
      Common 3D Printing Terms 19
    3D Carving for Patrons 22
    3D Carving for Staff 23
      Basic Process 23
      Information about Carvey 24
        Changing the bit 25
        Clamping material 29
        Troubleshooting 32
        Common 3D Carving Terms 33
  Digital Production 35
    Poster Printing for Patrons 36
    Poster Printing for Staff 38
    AV Equipment for Patrons 39
    AV Equipment for Staff 40
    Circuits 41
  Craft Fabrication 43
    Manual & Power Tools for Patrons 44
    Manual & Power Tools for Staff 45
    Sewing for Patrons & Staff 46
    Handcraft Tools for Patrons 47
    Handcraft Tools for Staff 47
      Button Making Process 48
Resources 50
Shift Tasks 53
Canned Email Responses 54
Team Schedule, Contact Info. & Log-in Info 57
  Log-in info 57
  Team Schedule & Contact Information 58

Figure 3.2 *Makerspace Employee Handbook*, table of contents, compliments of the American University Library Makerspace.

POST-CONSTRUCTION CONSIDERATIONS

Beyond the initial planning and design of a makerspace, additional opportunities exist for you, your makerspace, and the broader maker community. In this section we offer two such opportunities for you to consider. Because change is constant and the potential for improvement is ongoing, a post-occupancy evaluation provides a valuable moment of reflection. Likewise, while makerspaces may have shared characteristics and goals, each experience in planning and designing one is unique, as is the final outcome. Sharing your experiences and taking the opportunity to reflect on your learning benefit both you and others.

Post-Occupancy Evaluation (POE)

A post-occupancy evaluation is an opportunity to evaluate how the original goals for the space in terms of design have played out. A POE considers both aesthetic and functional aspects of the space and takes into account the actual activities happening in the space and how patrons are utilizing it. Approximately 12–18 months after final construction, walk through the space with the original planning documents in hand and assess, for example, where users of the space have relocated furniture and why this might be happening. Furniture and how individuals reconfigure it are often a good sign of deficiencies in a design and opportunities for improving it. Furniture may be relocated to access electrical outlets or to take advantage of views through windows or sunlight coming into the space. Likewise, furniture is often reconfigured to avoid drafts from HVAC diffusers. Other times, individuals might rearrange furniture to better support how they actually want to work within the space. If, as an example, you have provided beanbag chairs in a collaborative space but you find them pushed to the side and that other chairs have been brought into the space, it is a good indication that beanbag chairs are not supporting the type of collaboration happening in that particular setting. You might also find that additional furniture has been brought into a space to supplement what was originally planned. This is common in collaboration spaces and conference rooms. Such evidence is likely an indication that not enough seating or work area was planned for how the space is actually being used. The opposite may be true as well, with patrons moving furniture out of a space to make more room for how people are using the space. Once such evaluations have been made, appropriate action can be taken in the form of ordering additional furniture, swapping out more appropriate furniture for underutilized or abused furniture, or removing excess furniture to address how a given space is actually being utilized by patrons.

Another opportunity for evaluation is to review wear and tear of furniture, wall surfaces, and flooring. Check for things like furniture scuffs on wall surfaces, spills and stains on flooring materials, and the general cleanliness of furniture. Use of the space will be revealed through such evidence, and issues can be addressed before too much damage has occurred. For example, if you find that patrons are scuffing the wall surface with furniture, a protective rail could be added around the perimeter of the room to prevent damage from happening. Likewise, you might discover that flooring materials are not holding up against the patrons' use of the space. To address this, you may choose to step up the cleaning and maintenance routine or you may choose to swap out underperforming materials for more durable ones in order to maintain the desired appearance of the space. At the very least, you can begin to budget for such replacements and updates in the future.

Finally, consider utilization rates of both spaces and supplies. Assess whether or not spaces are active and being utilized as expected. This can be a visual survey, a head count, or an assessment of supplies in various areas of the space. If, for example, you never have to replace the filament for the 3D printers, it is a good sign that the 3D printers are not being used. If patrons are constantly asking for replacement dry erase markers for the collaborative space, it is a good sign that the space is popular. Utilization rates provide good evidence for future decision-making. If 3D printers are not popular, more assessment may be conducted to understand why. Perhaps training or workshops should be offered to help patrons feel more comfortable using such equipment or to showcase the opportunities that are available with 3D printing. Conversely, 3D printers may simply have been the wrong purchase and can be recycled elsewhere on campus, allowing that vacated space to be used for other equipment or for an entirely different purpose.

Post-occupancy evaluations provide an excellent measure of performance against the original planning and design objectives. It is not uncommon to find that such evaluations are never made because of time constraints, but, especially in spaces such as makerspaces, change is constant. There are ongoing opportunities to improve the space or alter it to match the reality of its use and evolving popularity. Later, in Chapter 6, we build on this idea and offer additional space assessment opportunities for you to consider.

CASE STUDY AND PRECEDENT STUDIES OPPORTUNITIES

Either at the conclusion of the construction phase or at the completion of a post-occupancy evaluation, consider submitting your makerspace experience as a case study for conference presentation. A range of presentation options exist at maker-specific conferences, general library conferences, and teaching and learning conferences, all of which may have an interest in your makerspace experiences. Many of the topics we have shared in this book could be translated into a presentation during which you share your experiences specific to your makerspace. The popularity of makerspaces continues to rise, and, as mentioned earlier, they are ever-changing. By sharing your story, you are providing a learning opportunity for others as well as opening yourself up for feedback toward continual improvement and the evolution of your makerspace.

Additionally, if you partnered with an outside design firm to design your makerspace, consider approaching them about case study, precedent study, and presentation opportunities. Not only are you helping others who may be interested in designing a makerspace, you are also likely to garner valuable feedback on the design of your space. Additionally, you are gaining notoriety for your makerspace, your library, and your institution for your innovativeness.

DIVERSITY AND INCLUSION IN MAKERSPACES

We want to conclude Chapter 3 by discussing a topic that has been alluded to in earlier sections: inclusive makerspace and goals of diversity and equity in the planning and design of them. As we discussed in Chapter 1, the mission of democratizing access is one just one example of why makerspaces and libraries are a natural pairing. Earlier in this chapter, we discussed practical planning tips and how such planning should take into account the needs and desires of diverse users. We encourage broad considerations because, as Soja (2010) suggests in *Seeking Spatial Justice*, physical space should not be viewed as neutral territory but rather as a reflection of those who create it. Often invisible but sometimes not, the forces that shape space, including politics and ideology, are at play.

To illustrate this point, Melo, in her keynote address at the 2019 Makerspaces for Innovation and Research in Academics (MIRA) conference, presented an analysis of *Make:* magazine covers across the publication's lifespan. Of the 64 covers, 37 featured people. Of those 37 covers, 76% were male and 14% were people of color. The importance of this fact is that *Make:* magazine was seen as the leading publication of its time for the maker community. The covers of *Make:* magazine were a reflection of their readership and likely a reflection of the diversity or lack thereof in the maker community. Melo (2019) further examined this reality by sharing an analysis of attendance data collected for the 2012 Maker Faire in the Bay area and the 2012 World Maker Faire in New York. As the premier maker events of their time, these two maker fairs had a combined attendance of 165,000 individuals, 66% of which were male. The median age of fair attendees was 46.5, while the median household income was $177,000. Ninety-eight percent of the 165,000 attendees had gone to or graduated from college, with 43% having obtained a graduate degree. Given the prominence of both the publication and the maker fair events in the maker community, it is not hard to imagine how diversity among makers has been shaped by such demographic realities.

If creating a welcoming makerspace is your goal, it is good to first revisit and clarify the terms involved: diversity, inclusion, equality, and equity. The National Education Association defines diversity as "the sum of the ways that people are both alike and different. The dimensions of diversity include race, ethnicity, gender, sexual orientation, language, culture, religion, mental and physical ability, class, and immigration status" (nea.org, para. 1). Beyond this, a broader understanding of diversity goes much further and recognizes that individuals are diverse because of their different experiences and exposures to life events, places, and people. Broadly, diversity speaks to the many ways we are different from one another. With this understanding of diversity in mind, inclusion is then defined as the goal of creating a feeling of welcome or belonging for people in all categories of difference (Bolger, n.d.). Finally, the terms equality and equity are often used interchangeably yet should be recognized as unique concepts. Equality, according to Davis & Harrison, "suggests that everyone should be treated the same, regardless of background, history, or needs" (2013, p. 24). In contrast, equity suggests that people be provided with what they need to have an equivalent experience or opportunity (Davis & Harrison, 2013). With these clear definitions in mind, we can then set out to explore further the ideas of creating such spaces and experiences.

Makerspaces and their use can be influenced by several forces, the first of which is who is in the makerspace. One of the first hurdles faced by CoLab, the collaborative space on the campus of Ohio University that functions as the hub in a hub-and-spoke makerspace model, was that much of the push for the space originated from the business college and its strategic efforts to support entrepreneurship. While perhaps not intending to dominate the space, the very presence of a high degree of eagerness to spur entrepreneurship was quickly perceived by others across campus and resulted in the space being coined a College of Business initiative. This perception was further legitimized by the fact that faculty from the business college held classes and meetings in the space after its opening to a degree not matched by other colleges or student groups in a sort of domino effect. This presence, both actual and perceived, influenced how others viewed the space and the likelihood of their using or not using it. Such influence can be perceived by others in a variety of forms. Everything from placing plaques that honor donors to the naming of a space can influence how we interpret the intent of a space and our belonging there.

Our feelings of belonging are also influenced by the activities that take place within the makerspace. A common example of this is how sewing machines are a trigger in makerspaces. Long-standing gender stereotypes suggest that sewing is a form of making practiced by females. Therefore, when sewing machines are present in a makerspace, they send a variety of subliminal gender-based messages to potential patrons. Male patrons may be turned off or discouraged from entering out of fear of being stereotyped as effeminate for using a sewing machine. Likewise, female patrons may be discouraged if they feel sewing machines reinforce undesirable gender stereotypes. Generally, the sewing machine may be judged as more craft oriented and the makerspace generally may be shunned by those seeking more hi-tech forms of making. Interestingly, while the marketing of a sewing machine in a makerspace may influence potential patrons, the visuals of the sewing machine can be influential as well. The dynamics suggested here may be entirely different if the model found in the makerspace is an industrial sewing machine versus a more typical home model. The type of sewing undertaken on an industrial machine and historic imagery of the industrial machine influence who will use it today and in the future. Such visual cues are important as they act as quick reference points for potential makers and their decision to engage with a makerspace.

Signage

Use signage or artwork to signal to the viewer an inclusive and diverse environment. Take note of individuals who are featured in the artwork, and strive to include individuals across lines of race, ethnicity, gender, culture, religion, and ability. Additionally, use phrasing in the visual communication strategy that tells the patrons of the makerspace that diversity and inclusion are valued. While words and pictures can only do so much, they signa to all patrons the values and mission of the makerspace.

Creating Opportunities

Be sure to provide a range of making opportunities as well. We will talk more about programming in Chapter 4, but specific to the planning and design of a makerspace, what tools and equipment are found within a makerspace also signal to the user who is welcome or who the space is tailored to. Along these same lines, be sure that the space is accessible for users with differing abilities. While the space planning will be guided by the Americans with Disabilities Act, for example, it should be noted that compliance with that federal mandate provides only the minimum of provisions for individuals with disabilities. Plan for varied or adjustable worksurface heights and spaces that allow for easy and inviting wheelchair access and that support collaboration across groups with varying physical abilities. Also consider how individuals who may have differing abilities with dexterity, stability, and mobility might access assistance in the various stages of making. Things like handles at surfaces to hold on to for stability, grip surfaces on tools, and furniture that can be leaned against for support are just a few examples of how a makerspace can be made to feel more welcoming and accessible by all makers.

Showcases and Displays

If you plan to incorporate a showcase or gallery in your makerspace, consider how that component of the design can be utilized. Displays or showcases can feature rotating makers and their work. This is an opportunity to be thoughtful about who and what is featured, being sure to feature makers across the spectrum of diversity. A popular direction in some making communities is to make assistive devices and prosthetics. One of the most powerful exhibitions of such making we have seen was *(dis)ABLED BEAUTY: The Evolution of Beauty, Disability and Ability* (Kent State University, n.d.), which featured assistive devices, adaptive services, and apparel of high design, all of which had been curated for the exhibition to reduce stigma and promote design across populations of differing ability.

Staffing

Along with how the space is planned and designed, you will also want to think about how making is supported in terms of staffing. Consider staffing the makerspace with individuals from across populations of race, ethnicity, gender, culture, religion, and ability. Staffing can include both paid and volunteer positions as well as both professional and student employees. This should also be considered when visiting artists, makers in residence, and workshops are hosted in the makerspace. When makers see others like them in the makerspace, it increases the likelihood that they will engage with the space as well.

In addition to the considerations above, Parker (2018) also suggests practicing *generous exclusion*. In this approach, excluding some individuals or activities makes others feel more welcome. In this practice, intentional boundaries are established that aim to support efforts of diversity, inclusion, and equity. It is important to note that in the practice of generous exclusion, three things must be clearly identified and acknowledged. First, decide who or what belongs and does not belong. Second, decide what is being undertaken in terms of activities from which individuals will be excluded. Third, clearly establish the purpose of such exclusion. These three steps will help to ensure that generous exclusion results in the desired outcome.

Ultimately, if your goal is to promote diversity and inclusion, you have to know the desires and needs of the individuals in the groups that you want to attract. Talk to them. Survey them. Find out why they are not coming to the makerspace. Ask them what their making interests are. Ask them how they might be encouraged to come to the space. Be intentional about creating spaces where diversity can thrive. It is important to recognize that we all view life through a lens of unique realities and experiences. In an effort to support and promote diversity, inclusion, and equity, you will want and need to consider the realities of other makers as they are experienced and perceived through lenses other than your own.

CONCLUSION

Grounded in a design thinking approach, this chapter has introduced practical considerations for the planning and design of a makerspace. From needs assessment to makerspace management, a successful strategy recognizes stated goals and desires but also attempts to anticipate unexpected realities. Pragmatic planning of a makerspace is also broad in considering not only the physical aspects of a space but also the recognition of people as an integral part of plan. While several makerspaces have grown from a more organic approach of simply providing resources and responding to the events that follow, a more intentional strategy from the start can help ensure success.

ADDITIONAL READINGS

Hamilton, M. & Schmidt, D.H. (2015). *Make it here: Inciting creativity and innovation in your library*. Santa Barbara, CA: Libraries Unlimited.

Kroski, E. (2017). *#the makerspace_librarian's sourcebook {*. Chicago, IL: American Library Association.

Moore, D.R. & Shoaf, E.C. (2018). *Planning optimal library spaces: Principles, processes, and practices*. Lanham, MD: Rowman & Littlefield.

Sannwald, W.W. (2016). *Checklist of library building design considerations*. (6th ed.). Chicago, IL: American Library Association.

REFERENCES

Bolger, M. (n.d.). What's the difference between diversity, inclusion, and equity? [Web log post]. Retrieved from https://generalassemb.ly/blog/diversity-inclusion-equity-differences-in-meaning/

Davis, T. & Harrison, L.M. (2015). *Advancing social justice: Tools, pedagogies, and strategies to transform your campus*. San Francisco, CA: Jossey-Bass.

Kent State University. (n.d.). *(dis)ABLED BEAUTY: The Evolution of Beauty, Disability, and Ability*. Retrieved from https://www.kent.edu/fashion/news/disabled-beauty-exhibit-opens-central-michigan-university

Melo, M. (2019, July). The possibilities and perils of inclusion in makerspaces. Keynote address at the Makerspaces for Innovation and Research in Academics (M.I.R.A.) Conference. La Verne, CA.

Nea.org. (n.d.). *Diversity toolkit introduction*. Retrieved from http://www.nea.org/tools/diversity-toolkit-introduction.html

Parker, P. (2018). *The art of gathering: How we meet and why it matters*. New York, NY: Riverhead Books.

Soja, E. (2010). *Seeking Spatial Justice*. Minneapolis, MN: University of Minnesota Press.

PART II

Strategies for the Library Makerspace and Broader Campus Initiatives

FOUR

Programming and Curriculum for Your Makerspace

It is essential to be intentional about developing programming and curriculum to encourage students, faculty, staff, and community members to engage with your library makerspace. Intentional programming and curriculum in the academic library makerspace can be leveraged to build powerful strategic partnerships and initiatives on campus that put the library at the center of broader campus goals, particularly those aimed at student success. In this chapter we explore how the academic library makerspace fits into the broader curricular and cocurricular missions of higher education. We review approaches to learning that are particularly conducive to the makerspace environment, discuss how making can complement information literacy, and explore programming that provides meaningful cocurricular experiences for users. We conclude this chapter by exploring various collections that may enhance programming and engagement with the academic library makerspace.

LIBRARY MAKERSPACES SUPPORTING THE CURRICULUM

The spirit of making is aligned with many popular curricular approaches today. The academic library makerspace supports active, collaborative, challenge-based, and project-based educational approaches. Indeed, Britton (2012) asserts that makerspaces support effective learning, acting as an informal space where students can enhance their learning experiences through informal, independent, or collaborative exploration beyond the traditional lecture model. This section provides an overview of these curricular approaches and offers examples of how to incorporate the academic library makerspace into the curriculum.

Learning Approaches

Makerspaces, generally, capitalize on approaching teaching as a facilitative and mentoring process. In the makerspace, students are encouraged to create and discover knowledge rather than receive it. Making activities are often collaborative and hands-on rather than rote, consumptive learning. Given that academic courses often still take place in a traditional classroom, an academic library makerspace can serve as a complement to more formal learning spaces. Students can apply traditional classroom content to expand, explore, and engage with material in the makerspace. Thus, the academic library makerspace can be a complement to formal learning intentionally tied to more traditional classroom curriculum or can serve as a space where students independently explore to enhance their studies.

While the library and its makerspace may not be able to directly affect pedagogical approaches across campus, being aware of contemporary approaches to teaching and learning can help library staff leverage their makerspace as a complement to the curriculum. Indeed, the academic library makerspace can be a second space where faculty and students can take learning beyond the bounds of the traditional classroom. Further, the opportunity for cross-disciplinary collaboration is heightened in the library space. The sections below introduce basic learning approaches to help situate the makerspace as a dynamic learning lab.

Self-Directed Learning

Makerspaces are wonderful places for students to engage in self-directed learning. Self-directed learning empowers students to create their own educational goals, set a course of action to achieve those goals, and helps them learn the processes and skills required to meet their objectives. The self-directed approach leverages our natural curiosity and desire to learn and grow (Gibbons, 2002). In the modern technologically driven workforce where skills such as problem-solving and creativity are paramount, self-directed learning within the academic library makerspace can be an excellent way to prepare students for future careers and lifelong learning. The freedom to explore a problem, investigate possible solutions, and proactively seek knowledge are valuable approaches to learning (Giuseffi, 2018).

Collaborative Learning

Makerspaces are particularly set up to promote collaborative learning. Collaborative learning, broadly defined, is an approach in which students interact with fellow students or faculty in joint learning efforts. Typically, the goal of the collaborators is to solve a problem, understand a phenomenon, or create a project. Collaborative learning calls upon a constructivist approach as collaborators create new or deeper knowledge together. The collaborative approach is thought to enhance learning because students seek understanding instead of receiving information or imitating others, similar to self-directed learning (Major, Barkley, & Cross, 2014).

Active Learning

Collaborative learning complements active learning by pushing traditional classroom boundaries beyond the standard lecture arrangement. Broadly, active learning moves students beyond being recipients of information via lecture to being engaged with the course content in a more meaningful way. Active learning focuses on the design of the physical classroom. Instead of rows of desks arranged like an audience around a stage, the active classroom includes tables for groups that promote discussion, brainstorming, and collaboration. Often, the tables are connected to digital technology to allow students to use digital resources and media to enhance their collaboration (Baepler, Walker, Brooks, Saichaie, & Peterson, 2016).

Project-Based Learning

Both active and collaborative learning approaches lend themselves to incorporating project- or problem-based learning. Project-based learning tasks students with solving a realistic problem. This approach empowers students to examine the problem to determine what they already know and what they need to learn in order to solve the problem and, in turn, establish a plan to successfully solve the presented problem (Amador, Miles, & Peters, 2006).

As demonstrated above, the academic library makerspace is a natural fit for collaborative, active, project-based, and self-directed learning. The library can leverage its makerspace to partner with faculty to help accommodate these approaches or can incorporate such approaches into library programming or information literacy instruction in the makerspace. The following section provides some basic ideas that can be expanded and tailored to fit the needs and opportunities on your own campus.

Library Makerspaces in the Curriculum

Perhaps the most basic way the library makerspace can complement campus curriculum is to include the space in the typical menu of subject liaison outreach. Subject liaisons can make faculty aware of the space and invite them to encourage their students to use the space to create class projects. Assignments can be paired with typical information literacy sessions that springboard to hands-on projects. Many courses now require students to go beyond the traditional research paper or slide presentation to create podcasts, videos, artistic works, and other deliverables for a class project. Regardless of the subject, the library makerspace can be very relevant to students by offering audiovisual equipment and software with corresponding workshops to learn how to use them. This is particularly helpful to students who find themselves required to complete a project but may not have access to or knowledge of the tools required to do so. It would be valuable, however, to hold an initial consultation with the makerspace manager, the subject liaison, and the faculty member to understand the assignment and to gauge training needs for the subject liaison, faculty, or students. Lesson plan collaborations among makerspace personnel, subject liaisons, and faculty are becoming increasingly common, and many examples can be found in the literature, at conferences, and online. The University of Texas at Arlington (UTA) offers a robust stock of example lesson plans on their website. See Chapter 6 for more information on the work UTA has done with lesson plans and related assessment.

Featured Makerspace: Carnegie Mellon's IDeATe@Hunt Making Facility

Carnegie Mellon University's IDeATe (Integrative Design, Arts, and Technology) makerspace is a true leader in incorporating making and innovation into the curriculum. Colocated in the library, IDeATe is coordinated through the provost's office.

IDeATe offers undergraduate minors and related courses in a variety of disciplines such as game design, animation and special effects, media design, sonic arts, design for learning, innovation and entrepreneurship, intelligent environments, and physical computing. The approach of providing interdisciplinary minors helps expand learning opportunities for students, allowing them to see how their work can complement other disciplines and how, through collaboration, they can push their shared work forward. For example, product development may require an inventor, a manufacturer, and a marketing expert, among others. The IDeATe curriculum helps students gain collaborative experience that will enhance their careers and foster innovation (Carnegie Mellon, n.d.).

The IDeATe approach also supports the greater institutional mission by supporting the type of innovation that can push the institution forward in scholarly activities while also serving as a tool to recruit high-performing students. Indeed, the admissions office features IDeATe in their recruitment material. The program has seen many innovative projects come to fruition that not only provide the student with invaluable opportunities to learn and develop, but also make meaningful contributions to technology and arts-based creative industries. Celebrated projects include subterranean music experiences in limestone mines, technology-enhanced gym ecosystems, a sound installation in a botanical garden, and creation of a robot to assist with postapocalyptic survival (Carnegie Mellon, n.d.). Explore IDeATe's web presence to learn more about the program, the makerspace, and the exciting interdisciplinary student projects initiated in the space.

Making and Information Literacy

Academic librarians are no strangers to information literacy instruction. Defined as the ability to "recognize when information is needed and have the ability to locate, evaluate, and use effectively the needed information," information literacy is central to making (American Library Association, 2019). In order to participate in ideation, tinkering, prototype iterations, and fine-tuning maker projects, the need for information must be recognized and effectively acted upon to inform the making process. Lofton (2017) makes a correlation between ALA's definition of information literacy and the making process. Lofton (2017) connects the recognition of the need for information to the ideation and brainstorming phases that can lead to finding and accessing necessary information to help guide how to do a project or solve a particular problem. Lofton also asserts that, as an iterative process, making and related information seeking, go hand in hand as a maker cycles through different approaches and methods, eventually settling on an appropriate solution for their needs.

Thus, information literacy and making can be seamlessly incorporated in both stand-alone information literacy sessions and as part of the broader making process. Information literacy instruction can be framed from a problem-solving perspective wherein students are presented with a discipline-specific or interdisciplinary problem. In the making environment, students are empowered to seek viable solutions to the problem using information seeking and literacy to guide their knowledge base, brainstorming, and ideation. For example, as Mann (2018) suggests, students can be presented with the challenge to address recycling behaviors on campus. Working through the project involves researching recycling bin designs, collaborating with classmates to work through iterations of brainstorming, building mock-ups, testing, providing and receiving feedback, and fine-tuning ideas.

Embedding making into information literacy instruction may build competencies such as creativity, communication, collaboration, digital literacy, technology skills, learning to cope with failure, trial and error, and learning how to use various tools and resources. Thus, embedding making in information literacy instruction may help expand and exercise skills not typically found in such instruction. Making helps bring the real world to information literacy instruction by expanding the need for information beyond the typical paper to implementing skills to solve real-world problems (Mann). Making can be applied to any disciplines, as explored below.

Business, technology, and engineering courses may be an obvious pairing for the academic library makerspace. Engineering courses often work with hands-on projects that involve tinkering, inventing, designing, prototyping, and testing. Engineering departments may also be well stocked with their own equipment-heavy makerspaces, workshops, and studios. The academic library makerspace, then, can be a space for ideation, brainstorming, and planning. Collaborative and contemplative space can help the project get going, while technology and audiovisual equipment can help bring an engineering project to a professional presentation, showcasing the work. Business courses, which often include group projects with elaborate presentations, could similarly make use of the space for collaboration, contemplation, and creating multimedia presentations to showcase their work. Likewise, science courses often take place in labs with highly specialized equipment. The academic library makerspace, then, can bookend work that takes place in a more specialized space on campus by serving as a space for initial ideation and feedback on iterations of the project.

Academic library makerspaces can even incorporate the arts and humanities to complement the broader campus curriculum. Librarians can partner with literature or composition faculty to design a collaborative project based on an issue or challenge described in a novel, short story, or poem. Students can engage with the literature in regular classroom discussion and paper-writing but could expand to include inventing a solution to the challenge or issue outlined in the book. This approach could work particularly well if faculty from different courses synced up lesson planning to cross disciplines. Faculty could bring students to the library makerspace where librarians could be on hand to assist with research while students make use of the space and resources.

As another example from the arts, music students could learn about the history and science of musical instruments through making. Understanding how woodwind, brass, string, and percussion instruments work could lead to making rudimentary instruments in the academic library makerspace. The culminating experience could be a display of the instruments, a musical performance, or an audio or video recording. For example, students could make diddley bows, a single-string instrument often made of repurposed materials. The instrument is a powerful way to learn about West African and southern African American music history.

Featured Makerspace: San Diego State University's buildIT

Jenny Wong-Welch (2019) at the buildIT makerspace at San Diego State University Library takes a unique approach to embedding information literacy instruction into orientation sessions for the makerspace. She shared her perspective at the 2019 Association of College & Research Libraries Conference. Wong-Welch views makerspace training as an ideal time to deliver information literacy instruction because students have self-selected to visit the makerspace because they are interested in the resource or have a specific project in mind. Wong-Welch believes interest makes the information literacy instruction more relevant and more likely to be retained. In order to make use of the equipment in the space, students must first complete an orientation and training. The training is performed by student workers using prepared slides. Training can take anywhere from 15 to 60 minutes, depending on the student's skill set. The training includes topics that tie to ACRL's *Framework for Information Literacy in Higher Education* (Association of College and Research Libraries, n.d.). For example, instructions for 3D printing include a discussion of using online sources while executing a project. The training helps students understand how to evaluate the source of the information and how to determine if it is a reliable source. Another example involves understanding that information has value. When exploring die-cutting technology, students may use an online source to find patterns to create a project such as designing a sticker. The software prompts the user through choices such as if you would like to pay a minimal fee for your pattern or use it for free. If you choose the free option, the pattern only comes in black and white and you are requested to cite the source of the work. This decision helps prompt a conversation about the value of information and how to appropriately cite sources. Wong-Welch views this approach as successful since at the time of her ACRL presentation, the makerspace had led over 600 students through the training.

Makerspace LibGuide/Resource Guide

LibGuides, Springshare's content management and curation platform product, have gained overwhelming popularity in academic libraries for creating webpages to guide patrons to targeted information. Even if you do not subscribe to a particular platform, providing a website or blog on which to provide information about resources and to highlight programming is invaluable. Information to include on the site includes location; hours of operation; a map of the space; a list of tools, equipment, resources, and collections available for use and circulation; circulation policies; community standards; general rules and guidelines; a calendar of events; and links to any social media. An online search for academic library makerspaces can help you find several examples of LibGuides and websites constructed to serve as an access point and information resource for patrons. All the featured libraries in this book provide excellent examples of makerspace web resources.

MAKERSPACE PROGRAMMING

The academic library makerspace can also serve as an invaluable partner to student affairs professionals who are engaged with developing cocurricular activities and engagement opportunities for students. The library makerspace can provide programming that complements student learning and provides an opportunity to explore new ideas and interests. Collaborating with student organizations, civic engagement groups, student affairs personnel, or community members can enrich your programming efforts. In this section we explore some examples of programming to draw students in to enhance their learning and development in and out of the classroom. First, however, it is important to understand a few grounding ideas in student affairs and student development literature. An understanding of concepts such as involvement, engagement, high-impact practices, and sense of belonging helps library staff create intentional and meaningful makerspace programming.

Student Development in Higher Education

In recent decades, higher education scholars have done significant work in examining student development and success theories. These theories ground many of the major initiatives on college campuses today. Likewise, these theories can be used to ground academic library initiatives, which can, in turn, complement broader institutional plans. Indeed, academic libraries can leverage their makerspace programming to promote student involvement and success. Before exploring specific makerspace programming and curriculum, we will briefly review the popular student engagement and involvement theories.

Involvement

Scholars such as Astin (1984), Tinto (1993, 2012), Kuh (2008), and Pascarella and Terenzini (2005) stress the importance of student involvement in curricular and cocurricular activities to promote student success. Tinto asserted that students who are engaged with their campus are more likely to be retained to graduation. Astin emphasized that a student's time is the most valuable institutional asset. However, Astin also advised that simply exposing a student to institutional resources is not enough, but that the quality, as well as quantity, of time spent engaged with the campus environment was important. Simply inviting the student into the library, then, may not be enough. Instead, quality services and outreach, such as academic library makerspaces, are instrumental for creating meaningful interactions. Makerspaces can be a nexus for what Kuh refers to as high-impact practices. Kuh provides examples of high-impact practices that increase student engagement and retention including common educational experiences, learning communities, collaborative assignments and projects, active and service learning, and capstone projects, all of which can include the academic library makerspace.

Sense of Belonging

Involvement not only bolsters the curricular and cocurricular experience, but also bolsters a student's sense of belonging. Strayhorn (2019) defines sense of belonging as: "students' perceived social support on campus, a feeling or sensation of connectedness, and the experience of mattering or feeling cared about, accepted, respected, valued by, and important to the campus community or others on campus such as faculty, staff, and peers." Thus, sense of belonging is a relatively emotional and relational way of making meaning of one's college experience. It is part of a greater and more complex framework of basic human needs (Maslow, 1954) and draws attention to challenges particular groups may experience in achieving a sense of belonging. Sense of belonging, then, is vital to effective involvement and engagement in curricular, cocurricular, and extracurricular activities. The library, and its makerspace, can play an important role in providing a welcoming, comfortable, safe, and supportive environment within which to connect, belong, grow, and learn. We will now explore programming opportunities to help foster a sense of belonging, engagement, and involvement in the academic library makerspace.

Events

The academic library makerspace provides a great opportunity to host events or to partner with campus colleagues for campus-wide initiatives. Events foster student involvement while raising awareness about the space and its resources. As you plan events, keep in mind regular campus-wide initiatives that you may leverage to enhance your own activities.

Campus-Wide Events

Academic libraries have become active participants in broader campus initiatives. Events to help kick off the new academic year or to help support students through finals have become quite popular. Events such as Welcome Week or Finals Week can highlight specific projects to promote engagement, awareness, or to relieve stress. These events are typically lighthearted and meant to promote library space and create a welcoming environment for students. Welcome Week events often include scavenger hunts, parties, or information fairs to help students get acquainted with campus resources, space, and staff. The library makerspace can play a role by hosting making events that help students decorate their dorm rooms or prepare for the semester. Creating banners, planners, or school spirit items are ideal for events that help students prepare for the new year. Finals Week events could feature stress-relief activities such as creating miniature meditation gardens. Even if the event does not feature making, hosting events such as therapy pets or mindfulness meditation sessions raises awareness of your space and may encourage future visits.

Library Events

The complementary approach to hosting events described above can be carried forward to events such as the popular Long Night Against Procrastination events often cohosted by academic libraries and writing centers. The makerspace can play a role by extending hours, providing increased staffing, or having themed sessions to help complete projects. Academic libraries also frequently host authors, artists, and notable alumni for speaking engagements. Often, supporting events will be planned based on the theme of the author's work. For example, a lecture on Lewis Carroll's *Alice's Adventures in Wonderland* may feature a visual arts exhibit, a book club talk, or a tea party. The makerspace could leverage these events to host maker events such as blending custom teas or decorating tea sets.

Independent Makerspace Events

The academic library makerspace can also host events that stand alone to feature the makerspace and foster the making culture on campus. For example, the library makerspace is ideal for hosting interdisciplinary events that highlight student and faculty innovation and creativity. Offering a regular speaker series that highlights making, creativity, innovation, or entrepreneurship provides a continuous opportunity for interaction among all disciplines on campus. See the Ohio University CoLab feature to learn more about events supported by academic library makerspaces.

Event Inspiration

The literature on library engagement events and maker projects is brimming with ideas. Projects can include a range of activities from duct tape crafts to digital wearables. Kroski (2018) provides an extensive inventory of projects in her book *63 Ready-to-Use Maker Projects*. Though the book is primarily geared toward the K–12 and public library audiences, many projects authored by contributors are a perfect fit for fun events for college students. Of particular interest are projects such as Jessica Logan's Create Your Own Lava Lamps and Magnetic Slime projects and Catherine Blair's Duct Tape Crafts project. The ever-popular trend of button making in libraries would also be a great small project to accompany any event. Consult the Additional Reading section of this chapter for resources that feature making and event ideas for libraries.

Exhibits

Exhibits are a fantastic way to showcase the work students and faculty completed while engaged with the makerspace. Exhibits may feature items, information, and interactive opportunities that highlight a specific theme or topic. Exhibits are often longer-lived and may require more coordination than events. Exhibits may be on display for several months, for a semester, for the academic year, or perpetually. There are several approaches to curating an exhibit. A permanent display case could informally feature small creations made by patrons. Curated exhibits that highlight making in different fields could expose patrons to the wide array of perspectives that find a home in the maker movement. Exhibits could be cocurated with academic departments to highlight coursework, senior thesis projects, or faculty innovations. Exhibits may be particularly attractive to faculty seeking tenure. Creating a network of potential and active collaborators will help your exhibits stay fresh and relevant.

A particularly impactful exhibit are maker-in-residence programs in which makers, innovators, and creators agree to "set up shop" in the library makerspace. Visitors may watch the maker-in-residence perform their craft, trade, or technique. Observing helps the visitor learn about the creative process, problem-solving, inspiration, or the particular process the maker demonstrates. The "in residence" portion of the exhibit could be complemented by lectures, workshops, and interactive events to enhance the experience. Potential partners for a maker-in-residence exhibit can be found by getting to know faculty, community partners, experts in the highlighted field, and students preparing for senior capstone experiences.

Civic Engagement

The academic library makerspace can be an important partner in civic engagement projects on campus. Events and projects can be organized independently or in partnership with other campus collaborators. Campus partners could include student affairs, student organizations and clubs, academic majors and departments, multicultural centers, LGBTQ+ centers, and women's centers. Campus partners can team up to serve local community organizations. Projects could include:

- Sustainability projects such as a recycling drive where participants can upcycle materials to create new items
- Creating scarves, hats, gloves, blankets, and supply bags to distribute to local homeless shelters
- Making toys for pet shelters out of recycled and upcycled materials
- Mobile makerspaces to provide the community with opportunities to create projects
- Solving a problem faced in the community

Regardless of the specific event, partnering for civic engagement particularly provides students with the opportunity to enhance their curricular activities with cocurricular involvement and service.

Featured Makerspace: American University's Bender Library Makerspace

American University's library makerspace grew organically. Initially, the space was a service-oriented facility offering large-format poster printing. Located in a modestly sized room on the library's first floor, the makerspace is expertly organized with an array of tools, resources, and supplies available. Faculty and students alike have taken to the space in exciting ways, and library staff have been eager to support their endeavors. For example, in conjunction with an anthropology of gender, sex, and culture class, one faculty member and their students used the makerspace to complete projects related to the course content. The students were able to pair making with service learning when they made reusable menstruation pads for a local organization. The class project accompanied discussions of the menstrual hygiene sales tax and gender equity issues.

In addition to their innovative faculty collaborations, American University's library makerspace has taken a unique approach to serving students. Library staff noted that the makerspace was popular among students who wanted to complete projects independent of their coursework. As staff interacted with the students, they learned that having an outlet to do crafts helped connect them to activities they used to do at home or with their families. Partaking in crafting in the makerspace allowed them to navigate feelings of homesickness and helped to relieve the stress of being a college student. Library staff began to view the makerspace as an important component to support student mental health and wellness. As one library staffer observed, "students are finding joy in childhood crafts." Particularly popular have been the sewing machines and related supplies. Given the popularity of hobby and craft interests, the library has offered an array of workshops, including photography and sewing, and special events, such as a drop-in event where students decorated their graduation caps. The crafting and stress-relief purpose inspired a series entitled Maker Mondays with the tagline to "Stress Less, Craft More." The Monday events are one-hour afternoon sessions aimed at relieving stress through crafting. Such events help foster engagement and camaraderie among students (American University Library Makerspace Facebook Group, n.d.).

Speaker Series

Offering a speaker series is an excellent way to bring campus and community makers together. Speakers can share their inspiration, process, technique, and how they successfully market, share, or kick-start entrepreneurial, innovative, or artistic endeavors. These themes apply to anyone, from writers and sculptors to computer programmers and business owners. Scheduling speaking events regularly over lunch or coffee can be a tradition that helps attract attendees who enjoy the social atmosphere. Ohio University's CoLab, for example, offers free pizza lunches at each speaker series event to encourage attendance. The weekly speakers are designed to focus on innovation and entrepreneurial spirit. See Ohio University's CoLab feature to learn more about the speaker series and extensive slate of complementary events.

Featured Makerspace: Ohio University's CoLab

Ohio University's CoLab opened in fall semester 2018 and operates under the hub-and-spoke model. CoLab offers spaces for ideation, collaboration, and feedback with a minimal stock of equipment. Instead of stocking a robust equipment inventory, CoLab serves as a connection point for users to branch out from CoLab to a wide array of makerspaces around campus, each with a unique focus grounded in specific disciplines. In order to publicize the space and encourage cross-disciplinary engagement, CoLab hosts an array of events, many of which are featured here.

CoLab has integrated into existing library events such as Welcome Week and Finals Week events. During finals week, students were invited to CoLab to make their own stress balls, visit with therapy animals, and enjoy a Relaxation Station in one of the collaboration rooms. CoLab also served as a resource for the Long Night Against Procrastination event traditionally cohosted by the library and writing center. CoLab provides complementary programming for other special events including Mom's Weekend each spring. While the library's Fine Arts and Special Collections areas offered bookbinding, CoLab partnered with a local community arts group to sponsor a make-your-own event. Known for their metal passion flowers and outreach to artists with differing abilities, Passion Works Studio provided premade metal flowers that students and moms painted together. Similarly, during Sibs Weekend, CoLab hosted an event where students and their siblings could make their own remote-controlled cars. Events like these make-your-own events can be great ways to introduce students to a space who may not otherwise have an opportunity to explore.

A Maker Fest or a celebration of student achievement can be an excellent way to showcase not only student work, but successful library and faculty collaborations in the curriculum. Having used the library makerspace as a bookend to their specialized work, students can participate in an event similar to poster sessions or academic fairs to explain their projects and network with students in other disciplines. CoLab held such an event in their library makerspace. Students prepared posters that were displayed on tables along with any other materials that they needed for display and demonstration. Similar to a poster session, attendees were invited to walk around the space and engage students in dialogue about their projects. Many student displays were collaborative projects. The event was a wonderful opportunity to showcase student work and demonstrate how the library makerspace can be a vibrant hub of cross-disciplinary making and collaboration.

Other CoLab events have featured experts and the process of making. One such event was the In the Key of Collaboration Event during spring 2019. Framed from the perspective of entrepreneurship and innovation, the event hosted a small group of musicians who provided a demonstration and question session. During the event, an acoustic songwriter circle was conducted to demonstrate ideas, skills, and creativity. This event was valuable in promoting the arts in a space that may have otherwise been dominated by business- and technology-focused activity. More information about CoLab can be found on the web (CoLab, n.d.).

Training Workshops

Academic libraries are no stranger to providing workshops that help students understand information literacy and research practices. Workshops in the library makerspace can be focused training sessions for the tools, equipment, and software available in the space. Likewise, the academic library can host workshops to introduce students to the network of makerspaces on campus including the library's own software, tools, and resources. Training workshops can help alleviate fear of unfamiliar resources and raise awareness of the equipment and tools available in the space. The University of Sydney's ThinkSpace provides a comprehensive program of workshops for all their technology.

Featured Makerspace: University of Sydney's ThinkSpace

Opened in August 2016, the University of Sydney's ThinkSpace, a technology-driven creative space, invites students to create, play, share, and discover by interacting with the resources in the space (University of Sydney, 2016). ThinkSpace provides students with 3D printers, a 3D carver, a programmable droid, virtual reality tools, a recording studio, computers, and workspace for design work. ThinkSpace is staffed by student workers known as peer learning advisors.

Recognizing that students may not have had the chance to learn how to use the resources elsewhere, ThinkSpace provides a comprehensive schedule of workshops to help students get acquainted and gain confidence with the equipment. The slate of workshops covers all the major technology in the space including workshops on Lulzbot TA6 3D printing, Carvey 3D carving, the One-Button Recording Studio, Oculus Rift virtual reality system, and Sphero, a programmable droid (University of Sydney, n.d.).

Once trained, the students use the equipment for fun projects such as creating small objects with the 3D printing and carving technology to complete class assignments using the recording studio. Workshops are regularly scheduled throughout the semester and are bookable online. The equipment itself, along with iMacs, Adobe Design Suite, and Wacom pads, are also bookable via the ThinkSpace website. ThinkSpace also facilitates connections via OzBerry, an online platform that supports online meetups to share projects, experiment with creative technology, and connect with people with diverse talents and skill sets. Set up as a Google group, OzBerry encourages communication and connection and spreads the word about monthly in-person hackerspace sessions (University of Sydney, n.d.).

The OzBerry monthly sessions are community-oriented events that focus on exploring various technologies such as Arduino, RaspberryPi, Beaglebone, Open WRT, Teensy, and Android. Participants are encouraged to bring works in progress to seek help with unfamiliar software, work through bugs, or generally be inspired. The sessions are 5 hours once a month and are open to anyone. The sessions include micro-talks on the hour and other speaker opportunities. The event also includes a flea market–style swap for equipment, giving students access to an affordable way to evolve their personal arsenal (University of Sydney, n.d.).

INCLUSIVE PROGRAMMING

Creating a makerspace that has inclusive spaces, services, and programming is paramount. Graves, Graves, and Rendina (2017) offer a robust list of tips to ensure inclusivity is a central tenet of your makerspace. Some of their tips are summarized below.

- Ensure that any advisory committees are representative of the student body. Students and faculty of various gender identities, cultures, religions, socioeconomic statuses, and other marginalized groups can provide valuable insight to create spaces and programming that are welcoming to all.
- Host events at various days and times, including lunchtime, evenings, and weekends, to allow students with all types of responsibilities and schedules to attend events. For example, parents may only be available nights and weekends, while students who pull double duty of coursework and employment may only be available during the day.
- Videoconferencing and streaming events can help students who are unable to travel to the makerspace or who may be nervous about participating an opportunity to be engaged in the events. Likewise, videoconferencing can expose students to diverse speakers who may not be able to make the trip or where funding to bring speakers to campus is unavailable.
- Likewise, social media can be an invaluable way to connect people and give voice to those who may otherwise be marginalized.
- Ensure furniture is accessible to all including tables of differing heights, aesthetics that can both stimulate and calm users, and that spaces are set up in ways that feel safe and welcoming.
- Offering a variety of workshops can help students choose in which settings they feel most comfortable. Smaller workshops can help students who are uncomfortable with larger groups, and targeted workshops such as women in STEAM can help empower participants.
- If your makerspace employs student workers, ensure that they are representative of the student body.
- Embrace all forms of making. Offer programming beyond the typical technology.
- Use makerspace programming to prompt students to think about tackling major issues in the world such as conflict, environmental concerns,

and health and wellness initiatives. Such projects can help students build empathy and understanding for people of different backgrounds and experiences.

- Likewise, using makerspace programming to expose students to other cultures can build empathy and understanding.
- When creating labels and signage, ensure that multiple languages are used. Pictures can also be beneficial as they transcend language.

Other considerations include:

- Be sure to take gender-inclusive approaches to programing.
- Ensure supplies are accessible to all abilities. For example, ergonomic pencils, pens, keyboards, and chairs for all needs should be available. Likewise, many tools are exclusive to right-handed individuals. Left-handed tools are an excellent addition to the space.
- Label colors for those who may experience color blindness.
- Arrange for sign language at events.
- Arrange for closed-captioning on all videos.
- Provide written, visual, and audio- or video-recorded instructions, rules, and policies.

FUNDING MAKERSPACE PROGRAMMING

Budgets for staffing, supplies, and resources may be one of the most challenging hurdles that library staff face in developing programming. Collaborating with internal and external partners can help overcome these hurdles. This section explores various methods to bolster your programming budget.

Donors

An innovative library makerspace could be a point of pride in conversations with donors and can open the door to small- or large-scale funding. Donors are often attracted to these types of endeavors because they are new, exciting, and on the cutting edge of creativity, innovation, and entrepreneurship. You may even offer your makerspace as a named donor opportunity. This can be particularly helpful in the beginning planning stages of your space. Donors may also be attracted to funding the purchase of equipment that relates to personal or professional interests. If your library has a Friends of the Library group, they may be an invaluable source for smaller-scale investments such as ongoing purchase of supplies or covering speaker or catering costs. Likewise, crowdsourcing is rising in popularity. Speak with your development officer to see if this is an option on your campus.

Campus Partners

Second, partnering with other offices on campus such as student affairs, student clubs, and other campus organizations may be a source of funding. Indeed, campus partners may have the desire to host programming, but limited funds to implement their ideal plans. Student affairs groups often have equipment such as popcorn poppers and cotton candy machines to enhance your events. Partners on campus may also be able to allocate staff or student employees to help plan and implement events. A collaborative approach also has the benefit of helping to spread the word about the value of the makerspace on campus.

Library Colleagues

Third, libraries often contain a wellspring of enthusiastic coworkers who are willing to participate in library events. Often, the library already has a standing outreach or programming committee, and makerspace programming can fit seamlessly into this workflow. You may be able to tap into these committees for volunteer help or to blend budgets to host programming or events. If your makerspace will have a dedicated staff member, that person can plan events and reach out to library colleagues to volunteer for special events. Library colleagues may also host information literacy initiatives in your makerspace. Regardless of the approach, a support system of enthusiastic library coworkers can bolster morale and help students and faculty get to know a broad range of library staff to increase engagement while saving money.

MAKERSPACE COLLECTIONS

From the print book to the electronic database to collections of physical objects, the academic library has always been the curator of the scholarly body of work and institutional and cultural archives. In many ways, the library's entire existing collection serves ideation, research, and making. This section highlights how libraries can develop collections to support the making process including maker-specific monographs and serials, works that inspire innovation and creativity, and collections of objects students can use both in and out of the space.

Maker Literature

If you choose to curate a collection specific to the makerspace, it may be worthwhile to develop a collection that complements, but does not duplicate, the general collection. The core collection can be supplemented with resources that outline the history and culture of the maker movement and contemporary themes in making such as innovation, creativity, entrepreneurship, and civic engagement. Practical guides to help bring making to fruition are invaluable resources to the budding and expert maker alike. Software manuals, trade publications, project ideas, and books on how to perform basic techniques in technology, arts, and craft can help makers put their plans into action and build their skill sets. Print resources can be stored on movable stacks that can pull double duty by delineating flexible space within a larger area. Electronic resources could easily be highlighted on the makerspace homepage or LibGuide. For a list of possible resources, please refer to the end of this chapter.

Tool and Technology Lending Library

Academic library and makerspace staff can help patrons gain access to expensive and specialized tools and technology to aid in project development and completion. A tool and technology collection can be especially beneficial if the library is unable to make structural changes to accommodate specific equipment needs such as ventilation and waste disposal. The lending system may particularly thrive in the hub-and-spoke model, in which patrons may begin their process in the central makerspace in the library and then transition to more specialized spaces within their discipline or field of interest.

Circulation policies for collection loans can be tailored to fit the appropriate length of time and replacement value of the equipment. The policy for the makerspace collections can fit seamlessly into existing integrated library system functions. For example, loan rules for peripherals or reserve items may already exist. Official circulation of all tools, even for in-room use, could be a practical way to ensure the security of the equipment and maintain statistics for assessment, late and replacement fee, maintenance, and reporting purposes. User agreements may be appropriate depending on the skill and risk level required. Power tools and sharper objects may require participation in a training workshop or signing an agreement that releases the library from liability for injury. You should consult with your campus legal counsel, environmental health and safety department, and design and construction office before purchasing equipment to learn which Occupational Safety and Health Administration (OSHA) standards specific to the use, operation, and installation of equipment and being used in the space, if any, apply.

Tools that may be useful in a lending library include:

- Basic toolboxes including hammers, screwdrivers, measuring tapes, and so on
- Sanders
- Routers
- Easels
- Sewing machines
- Sewing notions
- Glue guns
- Cameras
- Laptops
- Scanners
- iPads and relevant apps
- Knitting needles/crochet hooks
- Embroidery hoops
- Photo editing software
- Safety goggles

If budgets allow, providing consumable supplies for prototyping, tinkering, and brainstorming are also helpful. Such materials include:

- A variety of paper
- Markers
- Whiteboards

- Polymer clay
- A variety of pencils
- A variety of paints
- Paintbrushes
- Sketch pads
- Various sizes of sticky notes
- Pipe cleaners
- Popsicle sticks
- Glue
- Paper clips
- Rubber bands
- Plastic building blocks
- Cardboard
- Balsa wood

Reserves Collection

Riffing on a long-established library service, the academic library makerspace can explore how course reserves can evolve to support making in the classroom. In addition to traditional textbooks on reserve, academic library makerspaces can use equipment and supplies that are necessary to complete assigned course projects. This helps students gain access to necessary resources and acts as a means to formally or informally bring them together for collaborative work and community. Like traditional textbook course reserves, makerspace equipment and supplies reserves can also help reduce the financial barriers that students often face when purchasing class supplies. Working with subject liaisons can help you discover which faculty may be interested in placing various tools, supplies, or books on reserve for their course.

CONCLUSION

This chapter introduced an inventory of programming for your library makerspace. Programming in the library makerspace supports the curricular and cocurricular goals of the institution. From fun events to classroom projects and beyond, taking an intentional and vibrant approach to programming in your makerspace will help keep the space relevant to patrons. Developing collections to support your makerspace and programming helps patrons develop their skills as they learn to use the resources in your space. The next chapter explores themes of marketing and outreach to help advertise your programming and garner support for your initiatives.

ADDITIONAL READING

Alessio, A.J., LaMantia, K., & Vinci, E. (2015). *A year of programming for millennials and more.* Chicago, IL: American Library Association.

Bagley, C.A. (2014). *Makerspaces: Top trailblazing projects.* Chicago, IL: American Library Association.

Brejcha, L. (2018). *Makerspaces in schools: A month-by-month schoolwide model for building meaningful makerspaces.* Waco, TX: Prufrock Press.

Fleming, L. (2015). *Worlds of making: Best practices for establishing a makerspace for your school.* Thousand Oaks, CA: Corwin.

Graves, C. & Graves, A. (2017). *The big book of makerspace projects: Inspiring makers to experiment, create, and learn.* New York: McGraw-Hill.

Kroski, E. (2017). *#the makerspace_librarian's sourcebook {.* Chicago, IL: American Library Association.

Seymour, G. (2018). *Makers with a cause: Creative service projects for library youth.* Santa Barbara, CA: Libraries Unlimited.

University of Texas at Arlington. (n.d.). Maker literacies. Retrieved from https://library.uta.edu/makerliteracies/lesson-plans

REFERENCES

Amador, J.A., Miles, L., & Peters, C.B. (2006). *The practice of problem-based learning: A guide to implementing PBL in the college classroom.* Bolton, MA: Anker Publishing Company.

American Library Association. (2019, March 18). Evaluating information: Information literacy. https://libguides.ala.org/InformationEvaluation/Infolit

American University Library Facebook Group. (n.d.). Events. Retrieved from https://www.facebook.com/groups/aumkrspace/

Association of College & Research Libraries. (n.d.). *Framework for information literacy for higher education*. Retrieved from http://www.ala.org/acrl/standards/ilframework

Astin, A.W. (1984). Student involvement: A developmental theory for higher education. *Journal of College Student Personnel*, *25*(4), 297–308.

Baepler, P., Walker, J.D., Brooks, D.C., Saichaie, K., & Peterson, C.I. (2016). *A guide to teaching in the active learning classroom: History, research, and practice*. Sterling, VA: Stylus.

Britton, L. (2012). The makings of maker spaces, part 1: Space for creation, not just consumption. *Library Journal*, *137*(16), 20–23.

Carnegie Mellon. (n.d.). IDeATe: *Integrative Design, Arts and Technology Network: Heads together, minds open* [Brochure].

Gibbons, M. (2002). *The self-directed learning handbook: Challenging adolescent students to excel*. San Francisco, CA: Jossey-Bass.

Giuseffi, F.G. (2018). *Emerging self-directed learning strategies in the digital age*. Hershey, PA: IGI Global.

Graves, C. & Graves, A. (2017). *The big book of makerspace projects: Inspiring makers to experiment, create, and learn*. New York: McGraw-Hill.

Graves, C., Graves, A., & Rendina, D. (2017). *Challenge-based learning in the school library makerspace*. Santa Barbara, CA: Libraries Unlimited.

Kroski, E. (Ed.). (2018). *63 ready-to-use maker projects*. Chicago, IL: American Library Association.

Kuh, G.D. (2008). *High-impact educational practices: What they are, who has access to them, and why they matter*. Washington, D.C.: Association of American Colleges and Universities.

Lofton, J. (2017). Students are makers! Building information literacy skills through makerspace programs. *California School Library Association Journal*, *40*(2), 18–20.

Major, C.H., Barkley, E.F., & Cross, K.P. (2014). *Collaborative learning techniques: A handbook for college faculty*. (2nd ed.). San Francisco, CA: Jossey-Bass.

Mann, L. (2018). Making a place for makerspaces in information literacy. *Reference and User Services Quarterly*, *58*(2), 82–86.

Maslow, A.H. (1954). *Motivation and personality*. New York, NY: Harper and Row.

Ohio University. (n.d.). CoLab. Retrieved from https://www.ohio.edu/colab

Pascarella, E.T. & Terenzini, P.T. (2005). *How college affects students: A third decade of research.* San Francisco, CA: Jossey-Bass.

Strayhorn, T.L. (2018). *College students' sense of belonging: A key to educational success for all students.* (2nd ed.). New York, NY: Routledge.

Tinto, V. (1993). *Leaving college: Rethinking the causes and cures of student attrition.* Chicago, IL: University of Chicago Press.

Tinto, V. (2012). *Completing college: Rethinking institutional action.* Chicago, IL: University of Chicago Press.

University of Sydney. (2016, Sept. 2). Five reasons to visit the library's new ThinkSpace. Retrieved from https://sydney.edu.au/news-opinion/news/2016/09/02/five-reasons-to-visit-the-librarys-new-thinkspace.html

University of Sydney. (n.d.). ThinkSpace. Retrieved from https://sydney.edu.au/news-opinion/news/2016/09/02/five-reasons-to-visit-the-librarys-new-thinkspace.html

Wong-Welch, J. (2019). *The makerspace: A tool for information literacy instruction.* Presented at Association of College & Research Libraries 2019 Conference: Recasting the Narrative, Cleveland, Ohio.

CORE MAKER COLLECTION

The resources listed below aid in selecting materials to build a core collection for patrons as they explore various methods for making. You may need to consider the specific goals of your makerspace to curate a collection that is well suited to your library makerspace. Consider the supplies, equipment, tools, and technology available in your makerspace, and purchase resources that help patrons develop knowledge and skills to use the available resources. In addition, sources that generally focus on creativity, entrepreneurship, and innovation can inspire users.

Creativity, Entrepreneurship, and Innovation

Berger, J. (2016). *Contagious: Why things catch on.* New York, NY: Simon & Schuster.

Bornstein, D. & Davis, S. (2010). *Social entrepreneurship: What everyone needs to know.* Oxford University Press.

Chahine, T. (2016). *Introduction to social entrepreneurship.* Boca Raton, FL: CRC Press, Taylor & Francis Group.

Christensen, T. (2015). *The creativity challenge: Design, experiment, test, innovate, build, create, inspire, and unleash your genius.* Avon, MA: Adams Media.

DeGraff, J. & DeGraff, S. (2017). *The innovation code: The creative power of constructive conflict.* Oakland, CA: Berrett-Koehler Publishers.

Edwards, B. (2012). *Drawing on the right side of the brain.* New York, NY: Tarcher/Penguin.

Gibson, R. (2015). *The four lenses of innovation: A power tool for creative thinking.* Hoboken, NJ: Wiley.

Goldberg, E. (2018). *Creativity: The human brain in the age of innovation.* New York, NY: Oxford University Press.

Johnson, K.D. (2013). *The entrepreneur mind: 100 essential beliefs, characteristics, and habits of elite entrepreneurs.* Chicago, IL: Johnson Media.

Johnson, S. (2011). *Where good ideas come from: The natural history of innovation.* New York, NY: Riverhead Books.

Kelly, L., Walters, H., Pikkel, R., & Quinn, B. (2013). *Ten types of innovation: The discipline of building breakthroughs.* Hoboken, NJ: John Wiley & Sons.

Kleon, A. (2012). *Steal like an artist: 10 things nobody told you about being creative.* New York, NY: Workman Pub. Co.

Lefteri, C. (2014). *Materials for design.* London, UK: Laurence King Publishers.

Manzini, E. & Coad, R. (2015). *Design when everybody designs: An introduction to design for social innovation.* Boston, MA: MIT Press.

Neck, H.M., Neck, C.P., & Murray, E.L. (2017). *Entrepreneurship: The practice and mindset.* SAGE Publications.

Pacelli, R. (2013). *Whole lotta creativity going on: 60 fun and unusual exercises to awaken and strengthen your creativity.* CreateSpace Independent Publishing Platform.

Quibell, D.A., Selig, J.L., Slattery, D.P., & Moore, T. (2019). *Deep creativity: Seven ways to spark your creative spirit.* Boulder, CO: Shambhala.

Sharp, C. (Ed.). (2018). *The creativity project: An awesometastic story collection.* New York: Little, Brown and Company.

Shoup, K. & Gatski, K. (2017). *Starting an Etsy business for dummies.* Hoboken, NJ: John Wiley & Sons.

Tycho Press. (2015). *Etsy excellence: The simple guide to creating a thriving Etsy business*. Berkeley, CA: Tycho Press.

Wilkinson, K. & Petrich, M. (2013). *The art of tinkering: Meet 150+ makers working at the intersection of art, science & technology*. Richmond, CA: Weldon Owen.

How-To Guides

Bernier, S.N., Luyt, B., & Reinhard, T. (2015). *Design for 3D printing: Scanning, creating, editing, remixing, and making in three dimensions*. San Francisco, CA: Maker Media, Inc.

Bothmann, O. (2015). *3D printers: A beginner's guide*. East Petersburg, PA: Fox Chapel Publishing.

Ceceri, K. (2015). *Make: Making simple robots: Exploring cutting-edge robotics with everyday stuff*. San Francisco, CA: Maker Media.

Creative Publishing International (Eds.). (2014). *First time sewing: The absolute beginner's guide*. Beverly, MA: Creative Publishing International.

Davis, D. (2019). *Upcycled technology: Clever projects you can do with your discarded tech*. Coral Gables, FL: Mango Publishing Group.

Jackson, A. & Day, D. (1996). *The complete manual of woodworking: A detailed guide to design, techniques, and tools for the beginner and expert*. New York, NY: Random House.

Karvinen, K. & Karvinen, T. (2014). *Make: Getting started with sensors: Measure the world with electronics, Arduino, and Raspberry Pi*. San Francisco, CA: Maker Media.

Korn, P. (2003). *Woodworking basics: Mastering the essentials of craftmanship: An integrated approach with hand and power tools*. Newtown, CT: Taunton Press.

Louise, G. (2014). *How to get your product to market: A guide to design, manufacturing, marketing, and selling*. Great Britain: Harriman House.

Mongeon, B. (2015). *3D technology in fine art and craft: Exploring 3D printing, scanning, sculpting and milling*. Waltham, MA: Focal Press.

Moore, J.H., Davis, C.C., & Coplan, M.A. *Building scientific apparatus: A practical guide to design and construction*. (4th ed.). Cambridge, MA: Cambridge University Press.

Pakhchyan, S. (2008). *Fashioning technology: A DIY Intro to smart crafting.* San Francisco, CA: Maker Media.

Smith, A. (2018). *The sewing book: Tools, fabric, how to use patterns, projects for the home and to wear.* New York, NY: DK Publisher.

Stutz, M. (2004). *Linux cookbook.* (2nd ed.). San Francisco, CA: No Starch Press.

Williams, E. (2014). *Make: AVR programming.* San Francisco, CA: Maker Media.

FIVE

Advocating for Your Makerspace

Once you have established your makerspace and related programming, it is important to sustain interest in your space. Creating a culture of making and a buzz around your space will help raise awareness of what your makerspace has to offer and will help maintain interest over time. Likewise, building a population of engaged users helps to create a network of support to champion your space. If you are establishing a new makerspace, for example, you may want to hold a series of events to introduce your space, followed by a robust event and marketing schedule to sustain interest. Through these activities you may begin to develop relationships and ignite collaborations that will help keep your makerspace vibrant. Even with great success, however, come critics. Some may question the appropriateness of a makerspace in the library, the cost of implementing a makerspace, or misunderstand the value of a makerspace. It may become necessary, then, to respond to the skepticism. This chapter discusses how to market and advocate for your makerspace. The chapter concludes with a discussion of how to address the naysayers.

BUILDING A FRAMEWORK OF STRATEGIC SUPPORT

A vibrant community of support is essential to the success of your makerspace. Advocacy efforts raise awareness and build an ecosystem of support around your makerspace. Your advocacy may begin during the very early stages of planning your makerspace. Securing funding for your space may require appealing to multiple potential funding sources by demonstrating why your makerspace is worth investing in during a tight budget climate, for example. When advocating for new resources, it is imperative to tie your makerspace initiative to important library and campus values and projects. Developing a vision and mission for your space helps anchor your efforts in key initiatives in your library and on campus. Once you have secured support to establish your makerspace, you will need to help create a culture of making on campus. As you build buzz around your space, you can identify collaborators and champions to advocate for it. The sections below explore these themes.

Developing a Vision and Mission

Defining a vision and mission for your library makerspace is important because it establishes a focal point for makerspace initiatives and subsequent assessment. Your institution and your library likely have established vision and mission statements, which are commonly found on the respective websites. The institutional vision and mission serve as a guide to develop your makerspace mission and vision statements since you will want to ensure your makerspace supports the broader objects of the library and the university. This section defines vision and mission statements and offers examples and guidance to help you develop these statements for your library makerspace.

A vision statement typically takes an aspirational approach to describe the ideals of the organization. The vision is very forward-facing and defines future aspirations. Often, a vision statement will outline core values and establish future goals (Littler, 2005b). A vision statement is typically very short, often just one or two sentences. For example, an academic library vision statement may be, "The library will help faculty and students achieve scholarly excellence." Note that this example is a broad statement that positions the ideal of the library.

The mission statement carries the vision forward by defining how the organization plans to achieve its vision. The mission statement may define who the organization serves, what functions the organization performs in pursuit of its vision, and the purpose and responsibilities the organization holds in high regard (Littler, 2005a). The mission statement can vary in length, but it is advantageous to be succinct so that the intent is clear. A mission statement related to the above vision statement example might read, "The library will connect students and faculty with information that supports teaching and learning." Note that this example states who the library will serve and how they will help achieve the vision. The vision above suggested the library helps achieve scholarly excellence. This mission statement pinpoints that the library will achieve scholarly excellence by connecting students and faculty to information.

Your institution may also have a values statement. A values statement lists the characteristics that the organization strives to espouse. The statement often also includes definitions of the terms. For example, values that a library may find important are critical thinking, equal access, customer service, stewardship of knowledge and culture, and innovation. Examining the values statement of your institution and your library provides guidance on how the makerspace vision, mission, and values can be framed to support library and institutional ideals. Indeed, the makerspace vision, mission, and values should echo the library's vision, mission, and values, which, in turn, support the institutional vision, mission, and values. Searching online to find examples of institutional, library, and library makerspace statements can help you begin to brainstorm approaches, formats, and common language. The Citadel Daniel Library, featured below, does an excellent job of aligning vision and mission statements.

Featured Makerspace: The Citadel Daniel Library

The Citadel Daniel Library Makerspace provides an excellent example of how to establish a guiding vision and mission statement that aligns with the vision and mission of the library and the greater institution. For simplicity, the library and makerspace mission, vision, and values are presented here. The institutional vision, mission, and values can be found on The Citadel website (Citadel, n.d.). In brief, The Citadel institutional mission highlights a commitment to an intellectually challenging environment, teamwork, critical and creative thinking, the ability to apply abstract concepts to concrete situations, and using methodological skills to gather and analyze information (Citadel, n.d.). Below we present the Daniel Library's vision, mission, and values along with the makerspace vision, mission, and values. Brief discussions follow each. Notice that the overarching institutional statements lay the foundation for the library statements and, in turn, the makerspace statements. All statements are the work of the institution and are displayed on the respective websites listed in the References section of this chapter.

The Citadel Daniel Library Vision

> The Daniel Library and The Citadel Archives & Museum are the pride of The Citadel. The Library is integral to student learning, faculty scholarship, and the institution's ability to manage information and make decisions. The

Archives & Museum, as custodian of The Citadel's past and guide to its future, is an institutional treasure with a regional and national reputation. The Library and Archives & Museum are, to the students, faculty, staff, and alumni of The Citadel, the exemplar of information leadership, collaboration, innovation, and professionalism.

The Citadel Daniel Library Mission

The mission of the Daniel Library and The Citadel Archives & Museum is to deliver exemplary services for learning, decision support, and scholarship that inspire and excite our students, faculty, staff, administration, and alumni; to provide innovative information leadership to administrative and support units; to preserve The Citadel's unique and important information assets; and to offer noteworthy learning experiences and professional research services to Charleston, the Lowcountry, the state of South Carolina, and beyond.

The Citadel Daniel Library Organizational Values

We understand that our performance and behavior are guided as much by the spirit of the values as by the definition of the values.

Collaboration—We believe that the best possible results are achieved through partnerships and teamwork both on campus and throughout the scholarly community. True collaboration requires the inclusion of diverse perspectives and issues. It must also involve mutual respect and answerability. When the ideas and actions of all interested parties are considered, the whole is always greater than the sum of the parts.

Communication—We believe communication is essential to performing our mission and pursuing our vision. Communication is vital to building organizational trust and is the hallmark of respect. Communication is a multifaceted, mutually beneficial process, and the transformation of ideas is crucial to organizational advancement. We believe the initiation and articulation of ideas by people engaged in an honest, open-minded exchange result in new concepts, diverse perspectives, and organizational excellence.

Innovation—We believe that change is constant in a competitive and dynamic environment. At the heart of the truly innovative library are individuals embracing change, taking risks, and engaging with ideas beyond their comfort zone. Through the well-considered use of new models, practices, and appropriate technology, we can define the intellectual landscape and optimize The Citadel's leadership capability. Reflecting on and assessing innovative action also strengthens our ability to examine and improve our operations, services, and policies.

Leadership—We believe in principled leadership at both the organizational and the personal level. At the center of leadership is accountability for the responsibilities we have been assigned, and the ability to expand or enhance those responsibilities whenever possible. We believe that good leadership is characterized by the ability to make decisions, take risks, and manage failure. We believe great leadership creates an environment of inspiration.

Learning—We believe that learning is central to both our institutional function and our organizational identity. By expanding our skill sets and exploring new ideas, methodologies, and technologies, we can embrace an operational model based on the constant expansion of our experiential and intellectual horizons. We believe that learning from one another and sharing knowledge in a professional manner is vital to our daily operations and will determine the course of our future.

Professionalism—We believe professionalism is a fundamental value, and well-trained, knowledgeable employees are our greatest assets. Integrity, accountability, respect, and fairness guide our performance as we strive to exemplify professionalism in everything we do. (Daniel Library, n.d.a.)

The Citadel Daniel Library supports the institutional mission by highlighting "scholarship that inspires and excites students" and "noteworthy learning experiences." The library vision highlights the values of collaboration, communication, innovation, leadership, learning, and professionalism (Daniel Library, n.d.a.). These are all key themes that lay the foundation for the Makerspace vision and mission statements. The Citadel Daniel Library Makerspace Vision and Mission are posted on the library website and read:

The Citadel Daniel Library Makerspace Vision

The Citadel Makerspace is the center of new and emerging technologies on The Citadel campus, and a leader in educating Citadel students, faculty, and staff on how to explore and develop their creative and problem-solving skills in a collaborative and innovative environment.

The Citadel Daniel Library Makerspace Mission

The Citadel Makerspace fosters innovation, ingenuity, and creativity through the exploration of new and emerging technologies in an inclusive and collaborative environment. The Citadel Makerspace is a place where formal and informal learning come together to provide users with hands on experiences that help them refine their ideas, be more engaged with problem solving, and develop leadership skills, such as ingenuity, adaptability, collaboration, and persistence. The Citadel Makerspace is available to all active Citadel students, faculty and staff, regardless of their department or level of knowledge. (Daniel Library, n.d.b.)

The vision statement of the Citadel Makerspace establishes the space as a locus for the creation of new and emerging technology. The vision statement also highlights creativity, problem-solving, collaboration and innovation as important goals. The mission statement expands these sentiments by highlighting skills such as ingenuity, leadership, adaptability, and persistence. All of these are elements that tie directly to the library and institutional vision and mission statements. These key elements should be reflected in an assessment plan. More information on assessment can be found in Chapter 6.

Building a Maker Culture

Once you have established a vision and mission that support broader library and institutional goals, it is important to build a culture of making to help achieve the ideals and actions outlined in the vision and mission. Tying making to university and library culture will help establish making as a central component of institutional culture. For example, if the concepts of critical thinking, creativity, collaboration, and innovation are outlined in the institutional vision and mission, you should raise awareness about the ways your makerspace will help embed making in all campus initiatives.

You can begin building a culture of making by championing your space in meetings with campus constituents such as dean's groups, presidential advisory councils, departmental meetings, and faculty, administrator, or student senates. Casual conversation as you attend campus events is also a powerful way to keep your makerspace in the attention of campus constituents. Further, work to include making a part of regular library or campus initiatives. If your library hosts activities during finals week, ensure the makerspace participates with making activities. Alternatively, when campus events allow collaboration, think of ways to incorporate the library makerspace. If your campus hosts a day of service, for example, incorporate making activities that can benefit community organizations. You may wish to partner with other campus organizations that host service projects, such as fraternities and sororities.

Beyond spreading the word and participating in campus events, you can help encourage others to be empowered by making. Encouraging faculty to incorporate making in their teaching and research can build the culture of making in curricular and cocurricular pursuits. Offer grants to faculty to fund research, innovation, or to help reimagine their syllabi to include making. Likewise, university staff can play an important role in building a culture of making or innovation. Offer grants to support innovative ways to incorporate making in campus workflows or programming. All stakeholders on campus should feel included in the excitement of making.

Finding Your Champions

As you contribute to a culture of making on campus, you will likely develop relationships with students, faculty, and staff who can help advocate for the library makerspace. This can begin in the initial planning phases by creating a network of faculty, staff, students, and industry and community leaders who can help champion the value of making in the library. Once the library makerspace is established, your network can grow as more people interact with your space. This section explores ways to find your makerspace champions.

Ambassadors

A student may have overcome an academic challenge, a faculty member may have made important strides in research, or a staff member may have created a project that helps with their workflows. The users who become excited about your makerspace resources are excellent partners to help champion the space. Ask the excited users to serve as ambassadors to help spread the word of makerspace services and resources by providing firsthand success stories. The ambassadors can also help model behaviors that demonstrate how one can interact with a makerspace, helping to alleviate fear, skepticism, or intimidation for those who are unfamiliar with makerspaces. Include quotes or testimonial videos on your website or social media accounts. Such features not only provide content for your online media, but also honor the good work your stakeholders are doing that may be important to build resumes for future careers or to support tenure dossiers.

Advisory Groups

Establishing student and faculty advisory groups is a smart way to involve your supporters. Advisory groups help makerspace services and initiatives stay relevant as they play a firsthand role in guiding decisions and future planning. Faculty advisors can help you understand curricular and programmatic needs for teaching, research, and accreditation. Student advisors can help you understand the common challenges students face including necessary equipment to complete school projects or whether your open hours are sufficient. Staff advisors who work closely with students as academic advisors, student activities leaders, and residence life personnel can not only inform you of their own needs and wants but can also speak about students' needs and interests since they work firsthand with students. Finally, do not forget to include your library colleagues in advisory efforts. Since they share space and resources with your makerspace endeavors, they may have ideas on how to collaborate and create synergies that can benefit broader library initiatives. In addition to speaking with you about their needs and ideas, an advisory or volunteer group of library staff can help you with advocating for and communicating the value of your space to campus constituents. Indeed, building a core group of makerspace ambassadors can help support the culture of making.

Department Liaisons

In addition to building an advisory group, work with departmental liaisons to be introduced to faculty who may be interested in using your makerspace for personal research or in their courses. You can be introduced informally, during the liaison's departmental office hours, for example, or you may be introduced formally by attending departmental meetings. These meetings could lead to collaborations between makerspace personnel, subject liaisons, and faculty to create new assignments or conduct research. Connecting with student affairs personnel can also be fruitful as they work to enhance the student experience outside the classroom. Student affairs staff are always looking for innovative programming to support student engagement. If your library has an outreach or student success librarian, they may have established connections with student affairs personnel.

Hosting your own events to invite students, faculty, and staff into your space also helps to identify ways that they may engage with making. For example, consider hosting a series of open houses to promote the space. Each open house can target a particular audience such as campus leadership, faculty, staff, or students. Hosting an event for staff on campus may be particularly impactful as they may not frequently get the chance to attend such events. Indeed, staff members across campus can help champion your space as they advise and supervise students across campus. During your open house, conduct demonstrations or invite guests to engage in a making activity. For more innovative programing ideas, check out Chapter 4 of this book. West Virginia University's Sandbox, featured below, provides an excellent example of hosting intentional programming to raise awareness and build a network of champions.

Featured Makerspace: West Virginia University's TLC Sandbox

Taking a unique spin on the academic library makerspace approach, the TLC Sandbox at West Virginia University supports research and development for faculty, graduate students, and staff. The Sandbox is located in the Evansdale Library and is overseen by the Teaching and Learning Commons, a unit external to the library. The Sandbox offers collaborative furniture and an extensive list of technology including 3D printing, webcams, green screen, virtual reality, and a lightboard for course instruction. Complementing the Sandbox's array of technology options is an intentional approach to outreach and advocacy for their space. First, they offer Technology Integration Grants valued at up to $2,000 to full-time faculty. The intent of the grant is to encourage faculty to explore innovative and emerging technologies to enhance teaching and learning. Faculty are required to incorporate the new technology into their course to support learning outcomes, assess its effectiveness, and present their experience at a poster session at a campus event for faculty. In addition, the Sandbox hosts an annual open house featuring live technology demos to raise awareness about the resources available. The Sandbox also relies on formal and informal advocacy efforts. TLC personnel hope that faculty who have good experiences will share with other faculty and encourage them to use the Sandbox resources. More formally, the Sandbox website features video of faculty describing how to use resources and how those resources enhanced their teaching and learning. The Sandbox also organizes faculty advisory groups to inform about faculty needs and to provide peer-to-peer advocacy and guidance for Sandbox resources.

CREATING A MARKETING PLAN

Implementing a plan for marketing and outreach is another effective way to create a positive impression and help stakeholders understand your mission and values. Your library or institution likely has colleagues dedicated to marketing and public relations. It is valuable to establish relationships with these colleagues early as they may offer guidance for following institutional branding and marketing frameworks and can serve as valuable collaborators to champion your makerspace. This section helps you develop a very basic understanding of marketing to help guide your planning.

Building Your Brand

Branding can help make your makerspace resources and services recognizable. Your library and institution likely foster a particular image. It is important to consult with colleagues in the library and in university marketing and communications to ensure that you embody those values and visual style while also making your makerspace standout. Mathews (2009) explains that branding addresses three perspectives: visual, value, and emotional. The visual perspective is the set of images and look of your space and your marketing materials. Logos are the most obvious visual component of building your brand, but the visual appearance of the space can also play into the value and emotion of your brand strategy. Value has to do with how you would like the space to be perceived. This perspective attempts to help patrons understand why they should use your makerspace. For example, you may want patrons to think of expert support and an array of resources when they think of your makerspace. The emotional perspective addresses how you want patrons to feel in your space. Often makerspaces strive to inspire innovation and creativity. These perspectives are important to keep in mind as you build a marketing plan for your makerspace (Mathews, 2009; Potter, 2012).

Establishing Your Goals

Creating a marketing plan begins with defining your goals (Potter, 2012). Goals for your marketing plan should tie closely to your vision and mission statements and may easily connect with your assessment plan. Your goal may be as simple as to increase visitor counts, increase faculty course collaborations, raise awareness of your space, or attract new users, among many other possible goals (Potter). Measurable goals are best to aid in assessment efforts. For example, you may aim to increase faculty collaborations by 15%. Such a goal ties nicely with assessing the effectiveness of your operations as well as your marketing strategy. The assessment plan matrix in Chapter 6 serves as an excellent guideline for establishing your marketing goals alongside assessment goals.

Understanding Your Audience

Once you have established goals, it is helpful to understand your audience. Who are the specific target audiences for your space? Do specific academic disciplines incorporate making into their curriculum? Have certain majors yet to explore making? Are there community groups that may be interested in your makerspace? Understanding how to target outreach and marketing efforts to these groups can be a collaborative partnership with library colleagues such as the library's marketing liaison, outreach librarian, social media coordinator, web staff, subject liaisons, and public services staff. These colleagues can help you connect with various majors and departments and help craft effective targeted marketing (Potter). If your library has committees that focus on marketing, events, or outreach, it may behoove you to consider serving on those committees or reaching to strategic colleagues to develop your own makerspace marketing committee.

Choosing Your Methods

The next step is to undertake your marketing initiatives. Choosing appropriate methods depends on your target audience. If you wish to reach faculty, guest appearances at faculty meetings, paper mailings in faculty mailboxes, faculty e-mail lists, or personal visits from subject liaisons may be most effective. Faculty can even help with your marketing efforts by inserting your makerspace information in syllabi or mentioning the makerspace resources in class. If you are reaching out to students, social media, flyers in popular campus locations, or student e-mail lists may work best. Regardless of your methods, you should design messages and images that achieve your desired goals. Are you introducing the grand opening of your space? Are you seeking to raise awareness of the resources available in the space? Are you promoting a specific event or workshop? Some methods to consider are:

- Flyers or posters
- Brochures
- Bookmarks
- Featured space on library or university website
- Social media
- Faculty print mailings
- Faculty and student e-mail lists
- Table tents
- Stickers on coffee jackets at local coffee shops

- Commercials on campus radio or television
- Ads or feature stories in the student newspaper
- Features in campus newsletters
- Slides on library or campus digital monitors

Digital Marketing

Perhaps the most popular medium for marketing is digital marketing through a website or social media. Your makerspace web and social media presence should be in line with your library and institutional web and social media. Check with your library or institutional marketing, public relations, or communications personnel to learn about guidelines and content schedules. Your library may prefer you to use a particular platform to build your web presence or your institution may prefer specific colors. Keeping in line with these policies will help sustain good working relationships within the library and on campus.

Beyond your website, there are a plethora of web and social media platforms that can help you spread the word about your makerspace. Platforms such as YouTube, Facebook, Twitter, Instagram, and Pinterest are all popular ways to push content to users. These platforms can be used to promote services and events, host videos and tutorials, communicate success stories, and, most importantly, engage with your stakeholders. Each platform has its own policies and services, so be sure to explore the possible uses and regulations for each. For example, Instagram and Pinterest are great for graphic-heavy content such as pictures of events. Instagram, Facebook, and Twitter are great ways to advertise events and services. YouTube and Instagram host longer-form videos. When you are considering content, consider the intent of the platform and your goals. Are you sharing photos? Are you advertising an event? Are you providing access to a tutorial? Polger (2019) and Thomsett-Scott (2014) provide detailed guidance on choosing and using web and social media platforms. Refer to the Additional Reading section of this chapter to learn more.

It is important to remember, however, that social media platforms ebb and flow in popularity and new platforms are introduced regularly. No matter the type of social media platform, several common threads guide their use. Solomon (2013) recommends earning social capital with your followers. Earning social capital implies fostering goodwill by being an active and authentic member of the online social community. Social media is two-way engagement. Simply advertising your events or resources does not foster the two-way conversation. Be mindful to actively respond to posts or repost particularly interesting posts from your followers or other related campus organizations. Work with your library's social media manager to ensure the library social media feed often reposts or highlights your library makerspace. Posts that invite engagement are also worthwhile. Invite your users to post pictures of their recent projects or pose challenges or issues that makerspace users can work together to address. Offering prizes for posts can create a fun atmosphere for users.

Creating a Marketing Timeline

Creating a timeline for your marketing efforts is also helpful. You may wish to send different messages at different points of the school year, for example. An awareness campaign at the beginning of the semester to ensure new students and faculty are aware of the space and that returning students and faculty keep it in mind may be helpful. Then throughout the semester you may wish to strategically advertise various resources, services, and events. For example, if you are holding workshops, it may be helpful to do so when faculty are assigning specific projects that will utilize the space. Sitting down each semester or academic year to plan your events and related marketing can help you stay organized and help you have consistent contact with your audience. Alternatively, if you are preparing for the grand opening of your makerspace, you can begin building excitement even before the space is open. For example, you may host a live camera feed on your website of the building progress or post progress results on social media.

Assessing Your Marketing Efforts

Assessment is key to ensuring your marketing efforts were effective. Did you accomplish your determined goal? Did makerspace visits increase? Did you gain more faculty collaborations for course projects? Did you choose the right message and right target audience? What happened that you did not anticipate? Were budget and resources sufficient? What will you do differently in the future? It is important to reflect on these issues and to determine how you might better reach your marketing goals in the future (Polger, 2019; Wolfe, 2005). Chapter 6 of this book explains more about assessment.

ADDRESSING THE NAYSAYERS

Despite your best efforts, you will likely experience opposition or resistance to establishing a makerspace within the library. These concerns may stem from fear of change or new technology, from politics surrounding repurposing or allocating space, or from skepticism of the role of making on campus, among others. This section explores some of the possible concerns and how you might engage in dialogue to help ease the tension surrounding these topics.

Competing Budget Demands

You will certainly encounter questions and concerns about budget funds as you envision, implement, and sustain your makerspace. These concerns may come from both internal and external stakeholders with competing interests. Whether you are addressing internal or external concerns, it is important to situate your makerspace within library and institutional goals and missions. If your makerspace can help achieve student success goals that support funding streams from tuition or government sources, be sure to be prepared to clearly communicate those advantages.

Further, instead of taking a competitive or adversarial approach, think of ways that you can join forces to collaborate with concerned individuals. The contemporary higher education environment, with its budget woes and pressures to produce career-ready students, values collaboration now more than ever. The collaborative approach also fosters a culture of civility and teamwork, which will benefit your organization overall. Partnering to achieve a common goal may help foster support from those who were initially skeptical.

It also behooves you to prepare a detailed budget to demonstrate how you will effectively and responsibly expend funds. Outline costs for personnel, equipment, supplies, events, and programming. Be sure to list in-kind contributions like existing library personnel who will staff open hours, maintain the space, or supervise students. List any efficiencies you can gain from collaboration with library or campus colleagues. If you expect any potential benefits to alleviate costs, highlight those as well. For example, if you will be able to use equipment, supplies, or student employees to produce needed items for events or workshops, highlight the cost-saving feature in your budget.

Space Concerns

Along with money concerns, you may also encounter concerns about space. First, library personnel may have concerns about reallocating space originally used for another purpose to house a makerspace. Often, new space use in the library comes from retiring a former use for the space. In many cases, this may mean shrinking the footprint of the print collection. Since print books are tied so firmly to the nostalgia and history of libraries, repurposing space from collection storage to support a makerspace could be a contentious conversation. Efforts to decrease the print collection may be part of a broader initiative within the library to manage print collections in the digital age. You can call upon these larger efforts to explain your desire to allocate space to making in the library. For example, library budgets are increasingly being moved away from print resources and away from maintaining print. Likewise, off-site or high-density storage facilities may offer better environmental conditions for print materials while also freeing up space in the library for new purposes.

Stakeholders may also be concerned about the potential over- or underutilization of the library makerspace. A new, exciting resource in the library may attract new users to the library. This can be viewed as a positive effect of creating a makerspace in the library since encouraging students to visit the library may help them create beneficial habits to support their studies. Increased crowds may bring increased demand for custodial services, and patrons may be frustrated that the tools, equipment, or seating is not readily available during peak times. Planning ahead for busy times such as midterms and finals week will help overcome some of these challenges. Likewise, as stakeholders pass through the library and notice the space is empty, they may begin to doubt the value of the library makerspace. As with any space, there will be ebbs and flows. To help balance the perception of underutilization, regularly share usage statistics and photos of the space in use on social media and campus news outlets.

Concerns may also arise because the proposed use of the space does not align with traditional notions of libraries. For example, colleagues may be concerned about noise levels. This is not a new concern to contemporary librarians who work in libraries that are more diverse and open than libraries of the past. Libraries do still provide quiet respite for studying and reading, but also intentionally allow for more collaborative space that is abuzz with activity. Ensure that you have included in your planning ways to combat disrupting surrounding spaces. For example, soundproofing the space or ensuring that quiet spaces are not located near the makerspace are possible solutions.

Akin to evolving attitudes toward noise levels, it may also take some time for colleagues to feel comfortable with the presence of supplies, tools, and equipment related to making in the library. Just as some have concerns about food and drink in the library, similar concerns may exist for the supplies, tools, and equipment used for making. When designing the makerspace, ensure that you include finishes that allow for creativity and freedom to tinker. Flooring options that are easily swept or mopped and tabletops that can handle spills, heat, and sharp objects are easy to incorporate into your design. For example, cork and similar materials help protect walls from tacks and pins. Be sure you also collaborate with your campus health and safety department to ensure planning for equipment also includes addressing the associated code requirements. For example, venting and exhaust may be an issue with certain equipment and supplies.

You may also receive the critique that the space will not truly be used for making, but instead will be used as a glorified study space. You can engage in this conversation by offering the idea that quiet reflection and study informs innovation, creativity, and making. If concerns center on the idea that students may not expect making resources to be available in the library, be prepared to talk about how you plan to advocate for the makerspace and about any outreach efforts you have planned. Others may suggest that students have makerspaces, studios, and workshops accessible to them in their academic departments. While this may be true, often students need to complete projects for courses outside of their major or may be engaged in cross-disciplinary work. The library makerspace can help fill the gaps, providing a neutral workspace that fosters collaboration. Further, you may have designed your space to avoid overlap with spaces for making across campus. You may have employed the hub-and-spoke model, for example, that situates the library as the central connector within the broader maker ecosystem on campus. Finally, the library may have more flexible hours than other makerspaces available on campus. Libraries often have longer open hours than many other buildings on campus. Thus, the library makerspace may be addressing existing access challenges on campus.

Technology and Equipment Fears

When discussing the possibility of hosting a makerspace in the library, internal staff may have several concerns. Among those concerns may be a fear or wariness of technology or equipment. To address fear that stems from inexperience or lack of knowledge about the equipment or technology, offer several opportunities for your coworkers to express their concern and to gain experience. Often when tackling change or a new skill, it is valuable to just let your colleagues be heard and acknowledged. Understanding their concerns helps you better support them. You can learn their perspectives in face-to-face meetings or through anonymous feedback mechanisms such as online surveys.

Your findings may lead you to establish workshops exclusively for library staff to learn about the technology and equipment. How-to workshops can help address knowledge gaps, while safety training can help everyone to feel more comfortable and confident with the equipment. Establishing space-use policies and safety rules may also help alleviate concern over improper use of the space. Allowing colleagues to tinker and spend time in the space may also help them get acquainted with it. Additionally, a collection of how-to manuals can further support training and education about the technology and equipment in the space. Information about building collections to support academic library makerspaces can be found in Chapter 4 of this book.

All of the methods mentioned above are also helpful in supporting patrons to overcome equipment and technology fears. The first line of support, however, should be a knowledgeable and friendly staff. Hiring staff with related skills and experience is ideal, but if you cannot hire expert staff, the above-mentioned staff trainings are invaluable in providing staff with the skills necessary to successfully support patrons in the space.

Supporting Student Learning

Some colleagues may not understand how making supports teaching and learning. There are many talking points to offer in discussion with colleagues who have such concerns. First, making enhances learning by complementing students' current coursework. Makerspaces can provide space, resources, and technology to complete course projects. Making and project-based learning help students approach course content from a tactile perspective, driving home readings and discussions in class. Second, the makerspace enhances learning and development outside the classroom by allowing students to pursue their passions and interests (Brejcha, 2018). Students may not be exposed to programming, woodworking, or sewing in class. The makerspace allows them to explore these interests that may enhance their studies. For example, a fashion merchandising student may benefit from making an article of clothing firsthand. Third, makerspaces expose students to different approaches and disciplines that expand their knowledge and skills within their own discipline through serendipitous interaction with others in the space. Furthering the above example, a fashion merchandising student may learn from and build collaborations with marketing students, students who can sew, or students who can use design software. Fourth, making helps students develop skills that will be valuable in the job market including critical thinking, creativity, problem-solving, and teamwork (Brejcha). Today's job market often requires employees to work across disciplines to move projects forward. For example, designers and inventors may work side by side with accountants and marketing professionals. Fifth, making supports high-impact practices such as participating in learning communities, capstone projects, and undergraduate research (Kuh, 2008). These practices help bolster student success by creating a sense of engagement and enhancing student learning. Finally, makerspaces provide students with a low-stakes environment to make mistakes and learn from failure. When students are not worried about grades, they are free to take risks and try creative solutions until a problem is solved (Provenzano, 2016).

Resistance to Collaboration

There may be those who prefer to work independently and do not wish to engage in the collaborative nature of makerspaces. Individuals are certainly free to engage in the practices that work best for them. However, it is increasingly important to take advantage of opportunities to collaborate in order to address the challenges a contemporary institution of higher education may face. Providing cross-disciplinary space may encourage faculty to forge cross-disciplinary research projects or curriculum strategies. Likewise, as employers increasingly call for well-rounded job candidates, it is helpful to provide experiences that expose students to different disciplines that may contribute to innovation within their chosen discipline. The challenges of the modern workforce and research environments increasingly call upon multidisciplinary approaches to problem-solving and project completion. It may be helpful in the case of those skeptical of collaboration to engage in conversation about how collaboration may forward their own research or teaching agenda.

You may also encounter challenges with constituents that you partner with to establish and sustain your makerspace. For example, budget concerns, personnel changes, priority changes, or other factors may lead collaborators to discontinue their investment in the library makerspace. It may be worthwhile to consider establishing a memorandum of understanding with all partners and collaborators when establishing your makerspace or when pursuing new endeavors in the space. A memorandum of understanding can outline the responsibilities of each party and address what to do in the event that a party needs to withdraw from the agreement.

Negative Social Media Feedback

Anytime you enter into an online or public forum, you are inviting a conversation with your audience. Social media platforms typically have features that allow users to rate the organization, post to their public wall, comment on posts, or send a direct message to the page owners. When you receive negative feedback via your social media outlets, Solomon (2013) advises to determine which type of negative feedback you are dealing with. First, the feedback may be a straight problem, which is the easiest type of feedback to respond to. A comment or message about a straight problem is simply a report of something that went wrong during an interaction between the person providing feedback and library makerspace staff. For example, a makerspace worker may have been rude to the user. This type of feedback can be useful since it may help you identify and fix problems. Second, the comment or feedback may be constructive criticism. Constructive criticism points out a problem but goes on to offer a solution. This can be particularly helpful and is usually done in a tone that is less aggressive and provoking. Third, you may receive a merited attack. A merited attack is an instance when a patron may be angry, often to a higher degree than the incident the patron is angry about warrants. Though the sender of the feedback may be overreacting, this type of feedback nonetheless may help you identify an issue that is easy or worthwhile to address. Finally, the sender of the comment or feedback may be trolling. Trolling differs from a merited attack because the person providing feedback does not have a legitimate reason to be negative. Typically, a troll is seeking to provoke a response for the sake of creating drama (Solomon).

Responding to the types of feedback described above can often be upsetting and may foster a negative reaction from makerspace staff. Thus, it is worthwhile to have a plan of how to address negative social media posts in a communications and marketing plan. It is important to acknowledge, however, that if you have determined the negative post or feedback is from a troll, it is best to ignore the post. Solomon advises against deleting the post as the deletion may inflame the troll to post more. The exception to this advice is if the person has posted a narrative that includes hate speech or harassment. In the case of hate speech, the post should not only be deleted, but the person should be blocked from making future posts.

Generally, it is often best not to respond in the heat of the moment, so taking a few moments to center yourself may be helpful. However, it is important to respond quickly. Solomon offers several practical tips for addressing warranted negative social media posts. First, it is important to gauge if the issue at hand is consistent. You do not want to rush into changing a policy, procedure, or resource based on one person's feedback. Second, responding promptly will help someone providing genuine feedback feel heard and that you are taking their input seriously. Third, be sure to consider your approach. Formal language is usually not appropriate for social media. Often, those who are providing negative feedback want to feel they are communicating with a person, not an organization. Using a friendly and personable tone can make the feedback provider feel more at ease. In fact, the online environment may not be the best venue to communicate with the concerned party. Consider following up with a direct message in addition to a public post. Fourth, if you have confirmed a truly negative and unacceptable event has occurred in your makerspace, be the first to address it. Allowing others to post about it first invites misinformation and surrenders control of the narrative. Fifth, in your response, do not be defensive; and take responsibility, when appropriate. Being defensive does not help resolve the issue. If it is within your control to make it right, make that promise publicly. Last, if the feedback is warranted, take responsibility for making it right. Apologize first and show empathy to the person who provided feedback.

CONCLUSION

This chapter discussed various approaches to advocating for your makerspace including building a vision and mission, supporting a culture of making, advocating for your space, developing a marketing plan, and addressing the naysayers. Indeed, simply placing a makerspace within the library does not ensure it will attract crowds. It is essential to ground your makerspace within the values of your institution and then get the word out about the assets the space offers. One way to emphasize your outreach and marketing efforts is to support your claims with results of assessment practices. Chapter 6 explores building an assessment plan that demonstrates your value.

ADDITIONAL READING

Goodman, A.L. (2019). *Marketing plans in action: A step-by-step guide for libraries, archives, and cultural organizations*. Chicago, IL: ALA Editions.

Luttrell, R. (2018). *Social media: How to engage, share, and connect.* (3rd ed.). Lanham, MD: Rowman & Littlefield.

REFERENCES

Brejcha, L. (2018). *Makerspaces in schools: A month-by-month schoolwide model for building meaningful makerspaces*. Waco, TX: Prufrock Press.

Citadel. (n.d.). Mission statement. Retrieved from http://www.citadel.edu/root/mission-statement

Daniel Library. (n.d.a). Mission, vision, values, and strategic plan. Retrieved from https://library.citadel.edu/strategicplan

Daniel Library. (n.d.b). The Citadel Makerspace. Retrieved from https://library.citadel.edu/makerspace/policies

Kuh, G.D. (2008). *High-impact educational practices: What they are, who has access to them, and why they matter.* Washington, DC: Association of American Colleges and Universities.

Littler, D. (2005a). Mission statement. In *The Blackwell encyclopedia of management* (Vol. IX, p. 222). Malden, MA: Blackwell Publishing.

Littler, D. (2005b). Vision statement. In *The Blackwell encyclopedia of management* (Vol. IX, p. 381). Malden, MA: Blackwell Publishing.

Mathews, B. (2009). *Marketing today's academic library: A bold new approach to communicating with students*. Chicago, IL: American Library Association.

Polger, M.A. (2019). *Library marketing basics*. Lanham, MD: Rowman & Littlefield.

Potter, N. (2012). *The library marketing toolkit.* London, UK: Facet.

Provenzano, N. (2016). *Your starter guide to makerspaces.* Blend Education.

Solomon, L. (2013). *The librarian's nitty-gritty guide to content marketing.* Chicago, IL: American Library Association.

Thomsett-Scott, B.C. (2014). *Marketing with social media.* Chicago, IL: ALA TechSource.

Wolfe, L.A. (2005). *Library public relations, promotions, and communications.* (2nd ed.). New York, NY: Neal-Shuman Publishers.

SIX

Assessing Your Makerspace

Demonstrating value and assessing student learning and campus initiatives are salient themes in contemporary higher education. This, in part, is due to funding issues resulting from declining enrollments and the move to performance-based funding in many states. As departments on campus vie for scarce budget dollars, assessment of the academic library makerspace may be an important part of the library's story. This chapter contains information about the assessment movement in higher education and academic libraries, provides a foundation of qualitative and quantitative assessment methods, and shares how to communicate assessment results to champion your efforts and guide continuous improvement.

ASSESSMENT IN HIGHER EDUCATION AND ACADEMIC LIBRARIES

Assessment has grown to be a concept that encompasses many institutional efforts from student learning, to program assessment, to gauging the effectiveness and impact of a particular project, initiative, or service. Banta and Palomba (2015) define assessment as "the process of providing credible evidence of resources, implementation actions, and outcomes undertaken for the purpose of improving the effectiveness of instruction, programs, and services" (p. 2). Assessment can be undertaken for many reasons including accountability, improvement, and transformation. Academic libraries and their host institutions often must respond to external demands from accreditors and government officials as well as internal constituents such as provosts, presidents, and students. Assessment also has the power to address social justice issues by examining the experience of marginalized groups to improve services and address equity, diversity, and inclusion.

Many forces have pushed assessment to the forefront in higher education and academic libraries in recent decades. A push to tie higher education funding to performance outcomes began in the late 1970s. By the 1990s, an executive order was issued and renewals of the Higher Education Act mandated evidence of assessment for regional and disciplinary accreditation. Further, as state budgets tightened in the first two decades of the 21st century, the demand for assessment magnified as performance-based state funding was implemented throughout the United States. The performance funding zeitgeist has solidified retention and graduation rates as the ultimate goal of an institution. Thus, much assessment work done in higher education, particularly outside the academic disciplines, focuses on tying a unit's initiatives to how valuable those efforts are to support the retention and graduation of students (Banta & Palomba, 2015).

The rise of conferences, workshops, interest groups, and listserv discussions that focus on library assessment are evidence that academic libraries have taken the need for assessment quite seriously. Indeed, changes within libraries such as cost and evolving use of collections, services, and space have prompted academic libraries to rethink traditional statistics and assessments (Matthews, 2015). Academic libraries have increasingly begun hiring assessment librarians to help guide intentional assessment plans across the organization. Deans and directors use assessment data to champion library efforts to their provosts, presidents, and budget administrators. Indeed, the need to demonstrate library value has become a core pillar of the profession. Assessment in libraries is so embedded, in fact, that assessment activity is evident even before the external pressures of the contemporary landscape prompted the culture. A 2007 survey of 63 Association of Research Libraries (ARL) member libraries showed that the impetus for assessment for 91% of responding institutions was service oriented, user centered, and originated from within the library instead of external pressures (Wright & White, 2007).

DEMONSTRATING VALUE

In the past decade, library assessment efforts have amped up to fever pitch. This is due, in part, to Oakleaf's (2010) ACRL report *Value of Academic Libraries: A Comprehensive Research Review and Report.* In this report, Oakleaf defines value as a combination of return on investment and impact on the user. Oakleaf (2010) found that libraries often operate under the belief that they exist to support the institutional mission. Thus, assessment efforts at academic libraries may vary based on the primary visions of the home institution. Oakleaf (2010) challenged libraries to continue their existing assessment efforts, but to push to do more. Oakleaf (2010) encouraged libraries to define outcomes, gather data, create library assessment plans, and engage beyond the library by participating in campus-wide assessment efforts, engaging in professional development, and communicating assessment results to stakeholders (Oakleaf).

A key component of Oakleaf's work was to demonstrate the value the academic library contributes to student and institutional success. The 2017 report *Academic Library Impact: Improving Practice and Essential Areas to Research* provided a status report on the work done since Oakleaf's call to action (Connaway, Harvey, Kitzie, & Mikitish, 2017). The report offers guidance on how to effectively demonstrate library value. The authors suggest an impact agenda that is heavily collaborative. Though the report speaks to academic libraries as a whole, the report has valuable takeaways for academic library makerspaces. The report extends Oakleaf's original call to communicate value to stakeholders by quantifying the library's contribution to student success and communicating that data to stakeholders. Such communication can open the door for conversations on how best to tie library missions to institutional missions, how to incorporate library data with institutional data, and how to collaborate with educational stakeholders to improve teaching and learning (Connaway et al., 2017). Likewise, the academic library makerspace can coordinate with library assessment colleagues to embed the makerspace as an invaluable asset in the library's agenda to demonstrate its value. The remainder of this chapter helps those working with academic library makerspaces establish an assessment plan, connect with partners and collaborators, conduct assessment, communicate assessment results, and base continuous improvement on those results.

CREATING AN ASSESSMENT PLAN

In order to conduct intentional and strategic assessment of your academic library makerspace, it is helpful to develop an assessment plan. An assessment plan includes a framework for various assessment methods that holistically demonstrate the value and effectiveness of your makerspace program. In his book *Library Assessment in Higher Education*, Matthews

(2015) highlights four main phases of developing an assessment plan: planning, selecting assessment methods, analyzing data, and sharing results. In the first phase, planning, it is important to understand your stakeholders. This includes understanding the mission and vision of your institution and your library and the reporting and accreditation needs they require. The second phase includes selecting assessment methods and gathering data that captures activity that is important to you and your stakeholders. The third phase includes analyzing collected data to determine the impact of your space. This includes understanding library impact on such outcomes as student learning, teaching, campus innovation, and community engagement. The fourth phase of assessment planning includes sharing your results with stakeholders and reflecting on ways to improve your operations. This section explores the process of establishing an assessment plan for your space considering the steps mentioned above. For additional practical guidance for reflection on the assessment planning process, Oakleaf's (2017) *Academic Library Value: The Impact Starter Kit* is an excellent resource to consider as a companion to establishing your assessment plan.

Creating a Robust Plan

Before digging into developing your assessment plan, it is important to discuss rigor in assessment. Keeping rigor in mind throughout assessment planning can help build a robust and transparent assessment practice. In the book *Assessment Reconsidered: Institutional Effectiveness for Student Success*, Keeling, Wall, Underhile, and Dungy (2008) provide guidelines for building rigorous assessment practices. They stress that assessment must be transparent in purpose, values, positionality, and intent. This is particularly true when engaging with stakeholders. Keeling et al. (2008) stress that collaboration with stakeholders is essential to rigorous assessment. Collaboration with and input from stakeholders can help build a robust assessment program.

Next, Keeling et al. emphasize that the method chosen for assessment should appropriately reflect the questions being asked of the assessment process and should adhere to the common best practices of the chosen method. Finally, they advocate for ethical assessment methods, thus working with your institutional review board and assessment librarian are important. They also champion not only seeking answers to internal and external demands, but striving to contribute to the public good. Beyond assessing the effectiveness of your makerspace, consider the role your space is playing to promote teaching, learning, and research that improve our world.

Expanding on the concept of rigor, it is valuable to consider the validity and reliability of your assessment practices. Reliability refers to the consistency of the data produced by your assessment instruments. This means ensuring that all items within your instrument are written with the same goal in mind and that the resulting data is comparable. Improving reliability involves ensuring your instruments are well written so they are clearly understood. The length of the instrument should also be appropriate with the amount of time given to take it. Finally, it is important to ensure that those rating or analyzing the data are guided by the same understanding and interpretations.

Reliability is related to the concept of validity. While reliability speaks to the consistency of data over time, validity addresses whether the instrument measures what it is intended to measure. A well-defined purpose, transparency about interpretations, and justification of the chosen assessment method are appropriate for the intended outcome. As you develop your assessment plan, it is valuable to keep validity and reliability in mind to ensure a robust assessment practice (Banta & Palomba, 2015).

Understanding Your Stakeholders

It is important to have regular conversations with library leadership to ensure that the library makerspace supports greater library initiatives and can fit seamlessly into overall library assessment. Likewise, it is useful to consider how makerspace assessment can provide evidence for library leadership to advocate for the library makerspace to university leadership. For example, student retention efforts may be important to campus leadership. Library makerspace personnel, then, may find it valuable to provide infor mation to library leadership that demonstrates how the makerspace supports retention efforts. Tapping into the narratives used to champion the library provides a good roadmap to begin envisioning your assessment plan. Many of these campus narratives can be found in the library and institutional vision and mission statements. These statements are often prominently featured on the library or institutional websites. Likewise, reading through institutional and library annual reports and newsletters can clue you in to important campus initiatives. If your president or other leadership deliver an annual address, this can help you pick up on key themes and strategic pathways for your institution.

Engaging with faculty also provides invaluable input as many disciplines may have accreditation and programmatic needs that the academic library makerspace can help meet and, thus, provide an opportunity for collaborative assessment. Various academic programs may work with field-specific organizations that establish programmatic accreditation requirements. Often, these plans involve demonstrating the presence of library collections and services. This could be an excellent opportunity to partner with library subject liaisons to gain an understanding of programmatic accreditation needs and departmental missions. Additionally, faculty may require specialized tools, equipment, or space to support student learning to meet the goals of their accreditation projects. The library and its makerspace can partner with academic departments to help meet these curricular needs. Likewise, staying abreast of the latest developments and innovations within each field can help you identify and anticipate ways to support faculty teaching and research.

Before beginning your assessment planning, it is valuable to talk with your assessment coordinator or assessment librarian if your library has either of these positions. The assessment librarian or coordinator likely oversees the library's assessment plan and would be in the know about any standing assessment initiatives. Talking with the assessment personnel can kick-start your makerspace assessment plan as you may be able to capitalize on assessment methods and data collection already underway. Collaborating with assessment personnel can help guide your assessments to meet library and institutional goals and to choose appropriate assessment methods to achieve those goals. If your library does not have an assessment librarian, there are likely coworkers with an interest in assessment who can share what they have learned at conferences or from reading assessment literature. Institutional research and effectiveness offices are also valuable resources for assessment support. Do not be afraid to reach out to these offices for support or to inquire about collaborating on an assessment project. Often, institutional researchers welcome the opportunity to collaborate on projects outside their typical workflows.

ESTABLISHING ASSESSMENT CRITERIA

The next step in developing your assessment plan is to determine the criteria to be included. The criteria should be grounded in your vision and mission statements. Additionally, Matthews (2015) recommends considering purpose and the desired outcomes to guide your choice of assessment criteria. For example, consider if the focus of your assessment should be on such criteria as student learning, attitudes, behaviors, skill attainment, feelings, perceptions, opinions, or use. It may also be valuable to state goals or objectives in measurable terms. For example, the statement, "The academic library makerspace will increase student participation in innovative pursuits by 10%" can be used to guide assessments that highlight projects, inventions, or businesses that originated by using the makerspace.

When you establish a list of assessment criteria, consider the needs of your stakeholders. Use the information you learned from examining institutional and library vision, mission, and values statements and from developing your own makerspace vision, mission, and values statements to guide your list of assessment criteria. You may also wish to have conversations with subject liaisons and academic departments to understand what assessment criteria may be useful for them. Your assessment initiatives may include:

- Basic usage statistics
- Demonstrating how the space is used
- Demonstrating how the space supported an initiative or value important to the library or institution
- Demonstrating that activity within the space supported student learning
- Demonstrating how a partnership or collaboration supported institutional vision or mission initiatives
- Demonstrating the space contributed to a sense of student belonging or engagement
- Demonstrating satisfaction of patrons with programming, resources, or the space
- Demonstrating a contribution to faculty research

As you consider assessment criteria, it is imperative to keep the vision, mission, and values statements of the makerspace, library, and institution in mind to ensure that assessed criteria speak to values and initiatives of interest to stakeholders. Likewise, be sure that the assessed criteria are of value to the continuous improvement of the makerspace and the services offered. As you develop criteria, ask:

- Can the criteria be directly tied to a specific component of the makerspace, library, or institutional mission?
- Are the criteria of value to stakeholders (students, faculty, university administration, government officials, among others)?
- Can the criteria be used to improve makerspace policy, practice, or space?

With these values in mind, you can move on to determining the best method to gather data and analyze the criteria to be assessed.

Featured Library: University of Texas at Austin

In their article "Beyond Metrics: Connecting Academic Library Makerspace Assessment Practices with Organizational Values," Welch and Wyatt-Baxter (2017) offer a very comprehensive and practical approach to creating an assessment plan. The authors explain how their academic library makerspace, The Foundry, achieves assessment initiatives that tie to their mission. The Foundry employs an outcomes-based assessment model that grounds each successive step within previous steps. The components of the plan include identifying goals, outcomes, strategies, methods, and targets. Goals help to clearly and concisely unpack the components of the mission. Outcomes are measurable actions that describe how the goals will be achieved. Strategies, in turn, explain how the outcomes will be implemented. From there, appropriate assessment methods are determined and targets, benchmarks, or baseline goals for success are outlined. Welch and Wyatt-Baxter present a helpful grid in which to organize this information along with an illustrative example. Their method is an excellent way to organize your assessment planning.

DIRECT ASSESSMENT OF STUDENT LEARNING

When determining the appropriate approach for your assessment criteria, it is important to consider whether direct or indirect assessment will provide appropriate information for your needs. Direct assessment often refers to instruments and approaches that evaluate student learning first-hand. Examples of direct assessments are often performance-based initiatives such as exams, quizzes, portfolios, assignments, or journals. Direct assessment in the academic library makerspace requires students to complete an assessment of learning that took place using makerspace resources or spaces. It is necessary, then, to develop learning outcomes to be assessed. Such assignments can be incorporated into information literacy instruction or in collaboration with faculty in a discipline-specific or general education course. Assessment tools can be developed with discipline-specific faculty and can include rubrics, testing, or portfolios. The University of Texas at Arlington has developed a robust set of maker competencies to serve as inspiration for learning outcomes in direct assessment of student learning. See the Featured Library section below to learn more.

Featured Library: The University of Texas at Arlington Libraries

The University of Texas at Arlington (UTA) Libraries have been trailblazers in the academic library makerspace landscape. Funded in part by Institute of Museum and Library Services grants, UTA developed a set of makerspace competencies, dispositions, and values to provide a framework for aligning transferable skills achieved via making undergraduate curriculum. The strategic goal for the standards was to provide a framework for aligning transferable skills achieved via making with undergraduate curriculum. The competencies serve as an invaluable model for other libraries that are interested in collaborating with faculty to incorporate making into the curriculum. The competencies are "technology agnostic" in that they avoid naming specific technologies, which may pass out of fashion, become outdated, or may not be present in the makerspace. Instead, the competencies focus on cross-disciplinary, transferable skills that may be applicable to graduate school or future careers. The competencies are intended to assist faculty who may want to incorporate making into their lesson plans. With that goal in mind, the competencies are written as student learning outcomes. In addition to establishing a list of maker competencies, UTA has built an archive of lesson plans available freely online and are currently developing rubrics to better assess the attainment of learning outcomes. The competencies and the curriculum examples available on their website serve as a stellar guide for library staff to get ideas on who to reach out to on their own campus and the types of collaborations and assignments that are possible across the curriculum. UTA's list of maker competencies is reprinted below with permission.

The Maker-Literate Student:

1. Identify the need to invent, design, fabricate, build, repurpose, repair, or create a new derivative of some "thing" in order to express an idea or emotion, to solve a problem, and/or teach a concept
   a. recognize unmet needs that may be filled by making
   b. tinker and hack to learn how things are made and how they work
   c. evaluate the costs and benefits of making as an alternative to buying or hiring
   d. investigate how others have approached similar situations
2. Analyze the idea, question, and/or problem
   a. define the idea, question, and/or problem
   b. break the idea, question, and/or problem into its constituent parts
   c. question assumptions
3. Explore the idea, question, and/or problem and potential solutions
   a. garner input from stakeholders and peers
   b. research existing relevant products and ideas

   c. brainstorm a variety of solutions and pursue the most promising one
   d. evaluate the costs and benefits of using off-the-shelf parts or kits as opposed to making from scratch
4. Operate safely
   a. seek training and information on dangerous equipment and materials
   b. ascertain applicable technical standards and safety codes
   c. wear personal protective gear when appropriate
   d. reinforce safety precautions with others
   e. accustom self with location-specific emergency procedures, egress and disaster plans
   f. observe safety procedures in the event a person(s) is impaired or injured
   g. transfer safety principles gleaned in training to broader contexts
5. Assess the availability and appropriateness of tools and materials
   a. research various equipment and materials to determine limitations and suitability for a specific application
   b. choose the most appropriate tools and materials (physical, digital, and rhetorical) for the job
   c. acquire the necessary tools and materials
   d. investigate alternate tools and materials when a desired tool or material is not available
   e. fabricate necessary tools, reimagine material choices, develop alternate workflows, and/or revise project scope when alternative tools or materials are not available
6. Produce prototypes
   a. determine the method of creation most suited to the project
   b. gain confidence with technologies and processes required for creation
   c. specify functional requirements for prototype vs desired finished product
   d. divide design into individual components to facilitate testing
   e. document design process
7. Utilize iterative design principles
   a. apply measurable criteria to determine whether creation meets needs
   b. revise and modify prototype design over multiple iterations
   c. gather prototype feedback and input from stakeholders and mentors
   d. rework design to include insights from feedback
   e. take intelligent risks, use trial and error, and learn from failures

8. Develop a project plan
    a. identify who the relevant stakeholders are
    b. specify actionable and measurable project goals and requirements
    c. utilize time management and project management tools
    d. outline project milestones, including sequential action items
    e. anticipate time for multiple prototype iterations
    f. work effectively within project constraints, be they financial, material, spatial, and/or temporal
9. Assemble effective teams
    a. recognize opportunities to collaborate with others who provide diverse experiences and perspectives
    b. gauge the costs & benefits of "Doing-it-Yourself" (DIY) or "Doing-it-Together" (DIT)
    c. recruit team members with diverse skills appropriate for specific project requirements
    d. join a team where one's skills are sought and valued
    e. solicit advice, knowledge and specific skills from experts
10. Collaborate effectively with team members and stakeholders
    a. listen to others
    b. learn from and with others
    c. communicate respectfully and clearly with team members and stakeholders
    d. follow through on team commitments and responsibilities
    e. practice accountability both personally and with team members
    f. appraise contributions to the success of the team
11. Employ effective knowledge management practices
    a. restate technical and maker jargon for the layperson
    b. document steps clearly with sufficient detail for others to follow and replicate workflows
    c. use version control to manage project outputs and documentation
    d. preserve project outputs and documentation for long-term access
12. Apply knowledge gained into other disciplines, workforce, and community
    a. teach skills and share insights with other makers
    b. recognize and cultivate transferrable skills
    c. transfer knowledge, skills, and methods of inquiry across disciplines and activities

   d. familiarize self with skillsets of others
   e. connect those seeking to learn something with those who have relevant experience
13. Be mindful of the spectrum of cultural, economic, environmental, and social issues surrounding making
   a. express awareness of diversity and inclusion when identifying unmet needs
   b. consider sustainability when making, including upcycling and recycling materials
   c. scrutinize the ethical implications of making
14. Understand many of the legal issues surrounding making
   a. demonstrate an understanding of intellectual property rights and protections
   b. weigh the costs & benefits of seeking intellectual property protections v. making project outputs open and freely available to others
   c. examine the potential viability of both proprietary and open source systems to adopt/adapt
   d. respect the intellectual property rights of other makers
15. Pursue entrepreneurial opportunities
   a. perform thorough market research for competing products and capacity for monetization
   b. identify project outputs that may be protectable by trade secret, patent, trademark or copyright
   c. project costs of mass production and requisite economies of scale for return on investment
   d. refine financial plan for variable scenarios

Dispositions & Values

Makers:

- Construct knowledge and understanding through doing.
- Reflect on what they have learned by making.
- Convey curiosity about how things work, how things are made, why they have been made that way, and how they might be improved.
- Celebrate opportunities to share skills, knowledge, ideas, and creations to benefit a broader community.
- Practice persistence through the problem solving and iterative design process.
- Engage enthusiastically in opportunities to learn.

- Exhibit appropriate confidence in their ability to ideate, create, and problem solve.
- Embrace risk and innovation.
- Value collaboration and diverse perspective and experiences.
- Appreciate openness and sharing.
- Comprehend that the objects one makes are tangible forms of embodied knowledge.

INDIRECT ASSESSMENT OF STUDENT LEARNING

Indirect assessment methods may be easier to implement as they often do not require collaboration with faculty to assess student learning outcomes via a class assignment. Indirect methods are more reflective and often seek to understand perceptions or feelings to solicit testimony or opinion. Examples of common indirect assessment methods are surveys, interviews, focus groups, and other qualitative approaches. This section explores several methods to gather qualitative data as part of your assessment initiatives.

Surveys

Surveys are questionnaires administered to gather information from a target group with the goal to gain an understanding of their needs, behaviors, attitudes, perceptions, and opinions (Banta & Palomba, 2015). Surveys are also a convenient method to gather data at a relatively low cost. Further, surveys make it easy to gather information from large groups of people that you may not have the time or resources to meet with individually. Surveys can easily be administered using web-based tools such as SurveyMonkey, Survey Gizmo, or Qualtrics. Links to surveys can be embedded in solicitation e-mails, on websites, or posted on flyers with a QR code.

Surveys are ideal for gathering discrete data such as demographics and usage information including number of visits to the makerspace, which equipment was used, and what projects were completed in the space. Such data collection can result in standardized, robust data sets that can be used for analysis and data visualization. Surveys may also contain short, open-ended questions that explore how users value and experience the space. The responses can be used to understand nuances of user experience and identify themes. You may include closed- or open-ended questions in your survey, depending on your goals. Be careful, however, not to ask about multiple topics within the same question. Some example questions for a survey that explore student learning might include:

- Demographic information
  - Class (freshman, sophomore, junior, senior)
  - Characteristics such as international student, first-generation student, or gender identity, among others. Consider allowing the participant to select all that apply.
- Questions about space or resource use
  - How often did you visit the space to complete your assignment? A defined list of choices will help produce results that can be easily summarized. For example, if this question is left as an open response, you may get a range of answers such as: rarely, once, 3 times a week, or 2x.
  - What tools did you use to complete the assignment? Provide a list of tools and ask participants to select all that apply.
  - What equipment did you use to complete the assignment? Provide a list of equipment and ask participants to select all that apply.
  - How often did you ask makerspace staff questions during your last visit to the makerspace? Again, a defined list for the respondent to choose from is helpful.
  - Rate helpfulness of makerspace staff.
  - Was the environment conducive to completing your assignment? Why or why not?
- Self-assessment of learning
  - How did the makerspace assignment enhance your learning?
  - How did the makerspace resources help you complete your assignment?
  - What characteristics of the makerspace helped you be successful in this assignment?
  - What characteristics of the makerspace distracted from your learning?

  - Do you feel that you successfully achieved the stated learning objective? (You can specifically name the learning objective in your questions.)

Interviews and Focus Groups

Interviews and focus groups are excellent approaches if you would like to gather in-depth data from one person or a small group of people. An interview is a one-on-one conversation that is guided by a set of formal or informal questions. Focus groups are guided conversations with a small group of participants. The types of interviews that occur in one-on-one settings or in focus groups can be approached several ways. The interaction can be highly structured, semi-structured, or unstructured. In all cases, the interviewer enters into the interaction with a predetermined plan. In the highly structured interaction, a list of questions is set in advance, asked in a precise order, and, in some cases, may resemble a survey. The highly structured approach is best suited when you are trying to gather demographic data or usage data. In a semi-structured interview, the interviewer has a predetermined list of questions, but the questions are more flexible and open to conversation than in the highly structured interview. The order of the questions is also flexible, adapting as the conversation unfolds. The semi-structured interview is best when you want to explore opinions or perspectives but also want to be organized about the topics covered. Finally, the unstructured, or informal, interview is completely flexible. There may be a set of predetermined questions, but they may not be followed specifically. The unstructured interview is best as an exploratory approach where you may not be sure what you are attempting to learn and just want to generally learn about an experience or perspective. No matter your approach, opening the interaction with small talk or easy questions and topics can help the participant feel at ease and build rapport (Merriam & Tisdell, 2016).

Forming Questions for Surveys, Interviews, and Focus Groups

There are a variety of questions you may ask in a survey, interview, or focus group. First, demographic questions aim to gather basic information about the participants to better understand them as individuals and to build descriptive statistics of the population. Demographic data might include age, gender identity, race or ethnicity, or year of enrollment. Second, knowledge questions strive to understand the stock and quality of information known by the participant. For example, the interviewer might ask to what extent the participant knows how to use equipment in the library makerspace. Experiential, behavioral, or sensory questions seek to understand what the participant did or experienced from the step-by-step perspective to descriptions of sight and sound. For example, the interviewer might ask the participant to describe what they did during their last visit to the library makerspace. Third, opinion, value, or feeling questions seek to understand the participant's perspective. The interviewer may ask the participant to describe how safe or welcome they feel in the library makerspace (Merriam & Tisdell, 2016).

When designing survey or interview questions, it is important to not lead the participant toward a specific answer. The questions should be posed in neutral language that allows the participant to reveal their true perspective. For example, the interviewer should not ask, "How great is the 3D printer in the library makerspace?" Instead, a better question might be, "Can you tell me a little bit about your experience with the 3D printer?" Next, it is important to keep each question centered on one topic at a time. This will help keep the response focused and will set you up to have more organized data to work with. Finally, unless you are gathering demographic information, it is beneficial to ask open-ended questions that allow the participant to construct the narrative. For example, the interviewer might ask the participant to describe what they do during a typical visit to the makerspace, what challenges they encountered, what lessons they learned, how they use the space to support their coursework, what successes they enjoyed, or how they feel in the space. These stories can be especially useful when demonstrating value of the space to stakeholders. Student success stories can bring quantitative data and statistics to life and help stakeholders understand their impact in a nuanced manner.

Designing the Survey, Interview, or Focus Group

Regardless of the approach you decide to take, there are several considerations when conducting an assessment including seeking institutional review board approval, recruiting participants, and analyzing data. Whenever you are working with human subjects, it is wise to gain institutional review board approval. Your institutional review board will ensure that your assessment plan will offer proper treatment of your subjects. Institutional review board approval is particularly important if you plan to present your findings in a conference presentation, journal article, or book chapter.

Considering participants' comfort is key to fostering a good experience. The library is often an ideal meeting place for interviews or focus groups as participants are often familiar with the location of the building and may be familiar with the space. Study rooms or meeting rooms within the library or library makerspace are ideal for interviews or focus groups. When considering focus groups, it is important to be mindful of the demographic makeup of the group. Ensure that it is representative of the population. Typically, 6–10 participants is a manageable range for the interviewer and allows participants ample opportunity to participate. It is best for the participants to not be acquainted, though in a tight-knit library makerspace environment, this may be a challenge.

Another consideration for conducting surveys, interviews, or focus groups is how to recruit participants. Several strategies are available for this. You may post the invitation to participate on flyers around campus, post on social media outlets, or in a mass e-mail sent through campus mechanisms. Your institution may have an official procedure for sending a mass e-mail to all students or portions of students. Check with your institutional research, registrar, communications, or student affairs offices to see if such a service exists on your campus. Information to include on your communications are institutional review board approval, details about the goals of your assessment, any incentive you plan to provide, and how to contact you to indicate interest in participation. Small incentives are often effective in encouraging participants to work with you. If you do not have a budget to pay for incentives, consider grant funding sources or partnerships with other campus constituents or local businesses. Small denomination gift cards to the campus bookstore, dining hall, coffee shops, library printing services, or popular online vendors are quite desirable among faculty and students alike.

Conducting Interviews and Focus Groups

When participants respond to your call for participation, schedule the interview or focus group as soon as possible while enthusiasm for your project is active. Send a reminder before the scheduled time to help reduce no-shows. Ensure that the room is comfortable with appropriate seating. Having a bottle of water on hand is a nice courtesy. When you greet the participant be friendly and make small talk. You want to create a welcoming atmosphere where the participant is unafraid to share their perspective.

Begin the interaction with a few easy questions to help the participant gain confidence. For example, you might ask the participant to tell you about their major or what they are currently excited about in their college experience.

As you conduct interviews or focus groups, it is helpful to jot down notes to record the main points of participant responses and your own reactions and thoughts. It is important, however, to keep your attention primarily focused on your face-to-face interaction with the participants. So, while notes are helpful, it may be best to record the interaction by audio or video for later review and analysis. Your institutional review board will help you learn how to handle audio and video recordings. It is ideal to have the recordings transcribed for analysis. Transcribing recordings on your own is beneficial in helping you review and gain a deeper understanding of your data. However, transcription services such as Dragon and Rev.com are available as your budget allows. Transcripts can be used to code data.

Usage Data and Exit Polls

Usage statistics are often the low-hanging fruit of an assessment program. A sign-in sheet or card swipe system can record how often students visit, when they visit, and how long they stay. A card swipe system is particularly useful as it enables you to connect to institutional data. Increasingly institutions are purchasing tracking software to record tutoring sessions, advising appointments, and other academic activities to gain an understanding of what contributes to student success. The library can benefit by playing a role in understanding student success in this manner. Contributing library and makerspace usage data as part of the bigger narrative can help the library be an important asset to institutional success initiatives.

A manageable way to incorporate surveys into assessment of the academic library makerspace is to incorporate an exit poll. An iPad can be placed at the exit that quickly asks users which resources were used in the space, how long they stayed, or what type of project they worked on. Exit polls can also be used to gather brief demographic data such as major, class, or course. This information can help you understand which majors most actively use the space and which majors may be a good target for outreach efforts. You may also use card swipe technology to have users log into equipment and computers to understand how many times and for how long the resources are used.

SPACE ASSESSMENT

Another approach to academic library makerspace assessment is to examine the space itself. How is the spaced used? Is it used for its intended purpose? Have users revealed new uses for the space? Does the space have adequate furniture, equipment, and supplies? Does the design of the space foster the values you prescribed for it such as collaboration, creativity, innovation? This section explores various methods to assess space to explore these questions.

Surveys and Polls

Many of the methods that are useful in space assessment were introduced earlier in this chapter. Surveys, focus groups, and interviews are great ways to understand how patrons use the space. As mentioned above, simple exit surveys can be administered in print or electronically via a computer or iPad. The exit survey can be used to gather data about how long the patron was in the makerspace and the resources they used including particular areas of the space, equipment, supplies, or furniture. Having users swipe identification cards upon entrance and exit can also provide usage data as well. The swipes can reveal how long the user was in the space or provide a list of patrons to send a follow-up survey. The survey could ask the patron to reflect on their experiences and note the impact of their visit.

Whiteboard or bulletin board prompts can also be a quick way to gauge how the space is being used. Posting a prompt on a whiteboard, bulletin board, or even social media can be a quick and low-commitment way for patrons to provide feedback. Having markers, post-it notes, and stickers on hand can help patrons communicate their feedback. Some prompts may include:

- Please rate your visit today (Excellent, Good, Okay, Bad, Terrible).
- What do you like most about the makerspace?
- What new equipment/tools/supplies/services would you like to see in the makerspace?

More in-depth surveys can be administered by paper at point of contact within the makerspace. However, online surveys are popular due to the convenience for the survey taker and makerspace personnel alike. Survey takers can complete an online survey at their convenience with no obligation beyond responding and clicking a button to submit their answers. The survey taker accesses the survey via link embedded in an e-mail or web page. For makerspace personnel, survey data is already in an electronic format for easy analysis. Popular online survey tools such as SurveyMonkey, Qualtrics, Survey Gizmo, and Google Forms are all easy-to-use options that have built-in analysis features.

Interviews and Focus Groups

The results of surveys and polls may be helpful to inform more in-depth explorations through interviews and focus groups. Trends and issues uncovered in surveys and polls can be unpacked in conversation with patrons during interviews and focus groups, allowing for deeper understanding. If you note, for example, that individuals do not consider their use of the makerspace to be beneficial to their learning, questions can be designed to understand that perspective. For example, you may ask patrons to explain why they felt their use of the makerspace was not helpful. Was the needed equipment not offered or was it in use by other patrons? Was the assignment difficult to understand? Was the environment too noisy or too quiet? Was the furniture uncomfortable? Was the design of the space incompatible with group work?

Observation and Sweep Studies

Observation is another way to examine the use of a space. While surveys, interviews, and focus groups may help us learn about patrons' experiences in their own words, sometimes their responses may be formed by the interviewer's questions and reactions. Patrons may edit their responses or behavior when put on the spot or may forget important details of their experience. Likewise, participants may neglect to mention behaviors or information that have become routine for them. Observation helps to understand patrons through their revealed preferences and can provide context to interviews and focus groups. Certainly, the observer views the environment through the lens of their own experiences, but when combined with surveys, interviews, or focus groups, observation can be a helpful way to round out the full story. For example, you might simply sit in the makerspace and observe how patrons interact with the space, taking detailed notes of the activity in the space. You may observe how patrons travel through the space, which furniture pieces patrons gravitate toward, whether patrons sit alone or in groups, which collaboration rooms or areas are most frequently used, among any other observed detail. For example, observing multiple patrons leaving the space when they discover the area or equipment they desired to use was already taken by another patron can be very telling. Observing at planned times on a range of days can also help uncover rhythms of use that simple gate counts cannot express.

While observing, it is imperative to take a systematic approach. Push yourself to observe details you may not otherwise notice. Take descriptive notes that will help you recall and visualize your observations. It may be useful to have more than one person observe the same setting. This will allow you to compare and contrast the perceptions of each observer and fill in details that may have been missed. Some things to note include details about the setting, the participants, the activities or interactions that occur, and your own reactions and thoughts.

Another popular way to examine space is to conduct a sweep study to ascertain the occupancy and use of areas or rooms, furniture, equipment, and supplies. Sweep studies are often more methodical than observation and often involve recording how many people are using particular areas, equipment, supplies, and furniture in the space. Results are reported as statistics and occupancy rates. Graphics are helpful to show occupancy rate or use over days of the week or time of day. When designing your sweep study, you should consider what duration and timing within the semester are best. Ideally, you would perform a sweep study for at least a week to capture a full weekly cycle of use, but you can expand the study as much as you like. Be sure that you are situating the study in a time that is of interest to you. For example, you may want to examine use at the beginning of the semester or during finals week. Activity throughout the semester can look quite different, so schedule your study when it is most appropriate for you. Likewise, the frequency with which you perform the space counts depends on your needs and resources. You may count as granularly as every 15 minutes or only three times throughout the day. To ensure best results, however, whatever your frequency, you should do your counts at the same time each day.

Furniture Placement and Supply Inventories

If you have movable furniture, it can be quite telling to observe each day where patrons move the furniture and how they arrange it. Creating a map of the floor plan with prescribed furniture placement can be used at the end of each day to mark where the furniture originated and where it was moved. Furniture can be reset to the prescribed locations to observe how patrons move it each day. Is furniture moved to out-of-the way locations so students can have privacy? Is it grouped to allow for larger-scale group work? Are tables pushed together to create larger workspaces? All of these observations and more can be very helpful in creating an effective makerspace.

Likewise, supply inventory counts can help you understand what items are in high demand and at what times in the semester they are in highest demand. Begin by creating an initial inventory list and use it to conduct subsequent supply counts. You may wish to count daily if you are conducting a focused assessment of supplies, but weekly or monthly may make sense based on your needs and level of use. Timing of your inventories may be based on how often you need to order supplies. Regardless of when and how often you conduct inventory counts, doing so will give you valuable insight into what is popular and what types of activities are taking place in the makerspace.

ASSESSING WORKSHOPS AND EVENTS

Another assessment approach is to gauge the success of your workshops and events. These events may tie directly or indirectly to student learning or may serve other campus goals such as encouraging student engagement or sense of belonging. Beyond recording the number of collaborations, class visits, or events you host, it is important to assess the success of these activities. All of the methods mentioned above can be used to assess workshops and events, though surveys may be the most practical. Developing a brief survey for faculty collaborators to share if the use of makerspace workshops enhanced their teaching, research, or professional development can provide invaluable data. Likewise, gathering demographic information and a few brief questions on how a makerspace event or workshop enhanced a student's learning or college experience help you understand who is attending your events and provides useful qualitative data to use as examples demonstrating the value of the space.

INCENTIVES

For all of the methods described in this chapter, it may help to offer an incentive in exchange for participation in your survey, poll, interview, focus group, or other study. If the budget allows, small, inexpensive gifts may be purchased and awarded to all participants or a larger, more expensive prize can be raffled off. Even such small incentives as candy, library swag, or school supplies are popular. Collaborations with campus dining services, the campus bookstore, and local businesses are also quite popular. Dining services can offer free meal tickets, the campus bookstore could offer school spirit items or textbook gift cards, and local businesses could offer free food items. Partnering with local businesses in this manner can have the added benefit of helping students explore the surrounding community in ways they may not have considered or been able to afford. If a local community makerspace is available, they may be willing to offer free memberships or free event registration as an incentive.

RETURN ON INVESTMENT

In a higher education landscape increasingly concerned with budget, controlling costs, and demonstrating value, it may be helpful to frame your data in terms of return on investment. Considering your budget, grant dollars, or monetary gifts and how they directly tie to library use can be a good talking point for administration and to advocate for additional support. Whatever dollar figure is relevant to you, a simple return on investment calculation could include the dollar amount divided by a statistic that is important to you to get a cost-per-action statistic. For example, you could use gate counts, faculty collaborations, training session or workshop participants. An out-of-the-box way to think of return on investment perspectives is to offer stories of suggested projects, grades of students who used the makerspace for course assignments, and other qualitative data to go beyond simple return on investment calculations that focus on cost to focus on the impact the investment had on outcomes that may not necessarily be easily boiled down to numbers.

ANALYTICS OF MAKERSPACE WEBSITE AND SOCIAL MEDIA

It is important to acknowledge the digital presence of your makerspace. Are your website and social media presence effective? Are you meeting the goals you established? Website analytics and social media statistics can help you answer these questions. For websites, there are several factors to track including page views, visitors, time spent, page depth, and bounce rate. Page views let you know how many times each of your pages was viewed, helping you to identify popular content and to gauge if your website is functioning as you hoped it would. Page views do not give an accurate count of how many people visited your site, however, so recording unique visitors can help you understand the extent to which your visitors are new or returning guests. Page depth helps you understand how many sections of your site guests are exploring. Are they visiting a lot of pages or are they visiting just one page and leaving? The latter is counted in the bounce rate (Solomon, 2016). There are many tools to use to gather web data, but Google Analytics is perhaps the most popular. A free service, Google Analytics helps you understand how guests arrive at your site, how long they stay, which pages they visit, and how they exit the site.

Social media assessment can be a bit trickier. Each platform has varying levels of analytics, but standard measures include number of followers and engagement. Engagement includes the extent to which guests are liking, commenting, or sharing your posts. To go a bit more in-depth with engagement, you may wish to conduct a content analysis of comments in order to gauge whether they are largely positive or negative, what the common themes are, and which types of posts foster the most engagement.

ANALYZING ASSESSMENT DATA

Depending on your assessment methods, you may find yourself with a robust set of qualitative or quantitative data to analyze. Once you have completed gathering the data, you should select and implement methods for analyzing your data. This section provides an overview of basic methods for quantitative and qualitative data analysis.

Quantitative Data Analysis

The simplest way to analyze and present quantitative data is through descriptive statistics. Reporting total or average counts for visitors to the makerspace, attendance at events, circulation counts, or equipment usage statistics are effective ways to demonstrate how much your resources are used. Often, the data you present will describe an activity over time, such as data presented in annual reports. For example, you may report monthly total attendance or average workshop attendance.

Quantitative analysis lends itself well to data visualization. Presenting your data via chart, graph, or other visual representation may help stakeholders take in and understand your story quickly and effectively. Data visualizations can be created using Microsoft Excel or any number of other data visualization software programs such as Tableau. There are many online tutorials, webinars, workshops, and conferences offered in the library profession today on using tools such as Excel or Tableau to create data visualizations. Keep an eye on library listservs or conference program schedules to find data visualization topics that meet your needs.

Qualitative Data Analysis

Qualitative data goes beyond the numbers to help us understand the experiences of makerspace patrons. If you include open-ended questions in surveys or conduct interviews or focus groups, you will collect narratives that describe the experiences, opinions, or other information from those who participated in the assessment. If your respondents typed or wrote responses, the qualitative data is ready to use. If you are interviewing or conducting focus groups, however, you will likely make audio recordings of the interaction so that transcripts can be made for analysis. Whether your participants write their own responses or you create transcripts from audio recordings, you will have a stock of text that can be analyzed. You can pull quotes from this stock of narratives to emphasize positive experiences or statements that speak to the value your makerspace provided. Quotes pair well with quantitative data to help humanize the story your data tells. Quotes may also be used for promotional material or as captions for photos included in advertisements, posters, pamphlets, or reports.

If you have several responses from a survey, interview, or focus group, you can analyze the responses as a group to understand the main themes and popular points. Coding is a method for gleaning themes and trends from qualitative data. There are many ways to conduct coding, so you should consult several sources to find the approach that is right for your purposes. However, most coding approaches involve steps to read through the data to identify themes, key words, or salient points. Often, in a first read-through, the analyst will make notes in the margins to highlight the themes. After reading through all the qualitative data, the analyst may make a list of words or phrases that succinctly summarize the themes. It is useful to list all the codes and their meanings in a guide or codebook. The analyst may then read through the qualitative data and attach the codes to phrases, sentences, or paragraphs using color coding with markers or pens or by using software. NVivo or dedoose are accessible options for coding and analyzing qualitative data. Once all the qualitative data has been coded, the analyst can count which themes are most frequent and, in doing so, can begin to understand the popular themes from the group of participants. For example, if you are conducting interviews to understand how patrons value the makerspace, you may find that access to expensive equipment or space to collaborate with others are important themes among your stakeholders because they appear most frequently.

COMMUNICATING ASSESSMENT RESULTS

It is paramount to ensure that your assessment results, and your engagement with them, are shared with stakeholders. Keeling et al. (2008) provide guidance on how to make your assessment results relevant and sustainable. First, building a culture of assessment is particularly important. Assessment practice that fosters reflection, growth, and informs practice as a modus operandi will help sustain assessment efforts over time. Further, transparency in purpose and method is valuable to let stakeholders know the true intent and to assure validity and rigor. These values help align assessment with aspirational goals rather than maintaining the status quo. To that end, a robust program of reporting assessment results helps foster transparency, the culture of assessment, and continuous improvement. This section explores ways in which you may report assessment results to stakeholders to champion your makerspace.

Annual Reports

Annual reports are an excellent way to showcase your assessment results along with championing major events, initiatives, projects, and accomplishments for the year. Keeping a journal of your projects, events, and anecdotes will help you reflect on your year to reveal a bigger story. Keeping notes throughout the year is important. Without them, you may look back on your year and draw a blank and not realize the depth and breadth of your makerspace activity. Check with your assessment librarian or library administration to ensure that your report complements any library-wide or institutional annual reports. Share your report with library administration, campus stakeholders, and donor groups. Consider posting your report online so users can see the value of the space and to attract potential users. A convenient way to post assessment data and analysis online is to develop a dashboard. A dashboard is a concise, visual representation of statistics and information. The dashboard can serve as an excellent quick reference to tell your impact story.

Social Media

Social media and blog posts are another way to quickly share brief assessment results to foster a culture of assessment in your space. Posting stats or dashboards can help easily communicate quantitative data. You may also want to consider sharing qualitative data like success stories involving innovative projects and testimonials of how the space impacted student learning. Social media can also be used to gather data through quick polls or other engagement methods. See Chapter 5 for ways to use social media to spread the word about your makerspace.

Meetings and Campus Events

Getting on the agendas of key campus meetings is a great way to communicate your assessment results and initiate the conversation about your makerspace. Subject liaisons can present makerspace information and assessment data at faculty department meetings; or the dean or director can present findings to the provost, president, or other key campus stakeholders. Meeting with institutional research or the university marketing and communications departments are also great ways to embed makerspace data into wider campus communication and assessment initiatives. Campus events such as open houses and information fairs are great ways not only to raise awareness of your library makerspace, but also to provide concrete results of how valuable your space and services are.

CONCLUSION

As explored in this chapter, assessment is essential for demonstrating your value to your stakeholders and ensuring that you are creating a culture of continuous improvement. In order to demonstrate your value to stakeholders, you must understand their needs and interests. This can be done through conversation or studying the vision, mission, and values statements of your library or institution. Establishing vision, mission, and values statements for your makerspace that align with your library and institutional vision, mission, and values statements is also an essential task. Your assessment, then, can be grounded in the themes that are important to your library and institution. Identifying appropriate assessment criteria and methods can help you implement an assessment plan that is meaningful. Consider what you need to assess when considering assessment methods. You may be interested in assessing student learning, space use, or satisfaction with programming and events. Quantitative approaches are relevant when you need to gather statistics. Qualitative approaches are more appropriate when you need to dig deeper into opinions, perspectives, or experiences. A mix of both quantitative and qualitative approaches provides a balanced approach to reported assessment data. Regardless of your approach, it is important to build a formal plan with a timeline for implementation. Once your assessments are complete, you can begin the work of communicating the results to stakeholders and incorporating the findings into continuous improvement efforts. Communicating your assessment results to stakeholders is a major component to demonstrating your value to stakeholders.

ADDITIONAL READING

Andrews, C., Wright, S.E., & Raskin, H. (2016). Library learning spaces: Investigating libraries and investing in student feedback. *Journal of Library Administration*, *56*(6), 647–672.

Cun, A. & Abramovich, S. (2018). The challenge of assessment for library makerspaces. In *81st Annual Meeting of the Association for Information Science & Technology* (pp. 781–782). Retrieved from https://asistdl.onlinelibrary.wiley.com/doi/abs/10.1002/pra2.2018.1450550 1114

Danner, M.J.E., Pickering, J.W., & Paredes, T.M. (2018). *Using focus groups to listen, learn, and lead in higher education*. Sterling VA: Stylus.

Dobbs, A.W.T. (Ed.) (2017). *The library assessment cookbook*. Chicago, IL: Association of College and Research Libraries.

Dugan, R.E., Hernon, P., & Nitecki, D.A. (2009). *Viewing library metrics from different perspectives: Inputs, outputs, and outcomes*. Santa Barbara, CA: ABC-CLIO.

Evergreen, S.D.H. (2019). *Effective data visualization: The right chart for the right data*. (2nd ed.). Los Angeles, CA: SAGE Publishing.

Healy, K. (2019). *Data visualization: A practical introduction*. Princeton, NJ: Princeton University Press.

Hill, J. & Steffen, S.S. (Eds.). (2013). *Excellence in the stacks: Strategies, practices, and reflections of award-winning libraries*. Oxford, UK: Chandos Publishing.

Hillman, C., Blackburn, K., Shamp, K., & Nunez, C. (2017). User-focused, user-led: Space assessment to transform a small academic library. *Evidence Based Library and Information Practice, 12*(4), 41–61. Retrieved from https://journals.library.ualberta.ca/eblip/index.php/EBLIP/article/view/29312

Miller, R. & Hinnant, K. (2019). *Making surveys work for your library: Guidance, instructions, and examples.* Santa Barbara, CA: Libraries Unlimited.

Montgomery, S.E. (2013). Library space assessment: User learning behaviors in the library. *The Journal of Academic Librarianship, 40*(1), 70–75.

Morgan, D.L. (2019). *Basic and advanced focus groups.* Los Angeles, CA: SAGE Publications.

Robinson, S.B. & Leonard, K.F. (2018). *Designing quality survey questions.* Los Angeles, CA: SAGE Publications.

Wilke, C.O. (2019). *Fundamentals of data visualization: A primer on making informative and compelling figures.* Sebastopol, CA: O'Reilly Media.

REFERENCES

Banta, T.W. and Palomba, C.A. (2015). *Assessment essentials: Planning, implementing, and improving assessment in higher education.* (2nd ed.). San Francisco, CA: Jossey-Bass.

Citadel. (n.d.). Vision and mission statement. Retrieved from http://www.citadel.edu/root/mission-statement

Citadel Daniel Library. (n.d.). Vision and mission statement. Retrieved from https://library.citadel.edu/strategicplan

Citadel Makerspace. (n.d.). Vision and mission statement. Retrieved from https://library.citadel.edu/makerspace/policies

Connaway, L.S., Harvey, W., Kitzie, V., & Mikitish, S. (2017). *Academic library impact: Improving practice and essential areas to research.* Chicago, IL: Association of College and Research Libraries.

Gansemer-Topf, A.M. & Kennedy-Phillips, L.C. (2017). Assessment and evaluation. In J.H. Schuh, S.R. Jones, & V. Torres (Eds.), *Student services: A handbook for the profession* (pp. 327–343). San Francisco, CA: Jossey-Bass.

Keeling, R.P., Wall, A.F., Underhile, R., & Dungy, G.J. (2008). *Assessment reconsidered: Institutional effectiveness for student success.* International Center for Student Success and Institutional Accountability.

Matthews, J.R. (2015). *Library assessment in higher education.* (2nd ed.). Santa Barbara, CA: Libraries Unlimited.

Merriam, S.B. & Tisdell, E.J. (2016). *Qualitative research: A guide to design and implementation.* (4th ed.). San Francisco: Jossey-Bass.

Oakleaf, M. (2010). *The value of academic libraries: A comprehensive research review and report.* Chicago, IL: Association of College and Research Libraries.

Oakleaf, M. (2017). *Academic library value: The impact starter kit.* Chicago, IL: American Library Association.

Solomon, L. (2016). *The librarian's nitty-gritty guide to content marketing.* Chicago, IL: American Library Association.

University of Texas at Arlington. (2018). Maker competencies. Retrieved from https://rc.library.uta.edu/uta-ir/bitstream/handle/10106/27634/Revised%20List%20of%20Maker%20Competencies%20with%20Preamble-Corrected.pdf?sequence=5&isAllowed=y

Welch, A.N. & Wyatt-Baxter, K. (2017). Beyond metrics: Connecting academic library makerspace assessment practices with organizational values. *Library Hi Tech, 36*(2), 306–318.

Wright, S. & White, L.S. (2007). *SPEC kit 303 library assessment December 2007.* Washington, DC: Association of College and Research Libraries.

Conclusion

In this book we sought to provide practical guidance for implementing and sustaining academic library makerspaces. The unique perspective of both an interior designer and an academic librarian push the current, rich makerspace literature forward. The content presented in this book provided context to the broader issues surrounding making while also offering practical information to create or improve a makerspace in your own library. Ultimately, it is important to remember that making is a process that encompasses more than just the physical act. As such, when planning and sustaining a makerspace, it is essential to provide for contemplation and collaboration. Your makerspace should certainly contain equipment and supplies, but do not forget the context within which the equipment and making exist. This context includes the politics and red tape that come along with establishing and sustaining a makerspace in the library and the partnerships that requires.

As we close this practical guide, we encourage you to consider how to continue to elevate your space through broadening your perspective and thinking critically about your making practice. For example, we explored how the academic library is a natural fit for the making process. With access to information and space to apply knowledge and skills to create and innovate, the academic library and its makerspace can support wider institutional goals to support student success and faculty research and teaching. Indeed, library personnel must recognize making as a process. It is often easy to get excited about the latest fashionable equipment, such as 3D printing, but it is important to recognize that making transcends equipment. Making involves absorbing new knowledge, critically examining new information, forming new ideas, prototyping models, testing ideas, making mistakes, trying new things, collaborating, and giving and receiving feedback. Making is an iterative and multistep process. As you develop and sustain your space, remember to keep the whole process in mind to foster a holistic approach to making.

It is also imperative to think about how your makerspace can help achieve social justice goals. Makerspaces often join libraries in the important work of democratizing access to information and resources. It is important, however, to think critically about our spaces, resources, and services to ensure they are truly welcoming and equitable. Inequality in higher education persists, and students often face racial, gender, and socioeconomic challenges that affect their use of and access to spaces and resources. When we talk or write about making and makerspaces, it is easy to envision a utopia where makers are free to explore and pursue their interests. It is important to remember, though, that being present in a makerspace is a privilege that may be challenging for some users. For example, students may not have been exposed to practices that built confidence in the academic setting in their formative years. Other students may face time constraints related to the socioeconomic need to work or to family obligations. As you build and sustain your space, consider how privilege, or lack thereof, may have affected your potential users and work to be mindful of these differences in your practice. Likewise, helping students of all backgrounds and abilities feel welcome in the space is essential to foster a sense of belonging. Establishing codes of conduct or community standards to help guide appropriate behavior and treatment of others may be a valuable tool for your makerspace if such policies do not already exist in your library.

We hope this book will serve as a valuable resource to you on your makerspace journey. With the context and guidance this book provides, you will be well suited to create a holistic space that goes beyond equipment to consider the broader ecosystem that includes your makerspace, your library, and your campus environment. Fostering relationships in and around your space using the techniques in this book will provide a meaningful experience for your users and your institution. Indeed, fostering a vibrant makerspace in the academic library can enrich broader campus goals, solidifying the value of your space to faculty, students, and other stakeholders.

Index

About the Authors

KATY B. MATHUEWS, MA, MLIS, PhD, is head of collections assessment at Ohio University's main campus. She is an executive board member of the Academic Library Association of Ohio, serving as its president in 2019–2020. Mathuews has authored over 20 scholarly and professional publications. Her research interests include academic library assessment, academic libraries' contribution to student success, library space, and understanding and supporting marginalized student groups. She has presented her work nationally and internationally at many conferences.

DANIEL J. HARPER, MID, PhD, is assistant professor of interior architecture at Ohio University. Following a nearly two decades–long career as a practicing designer, Harper has held various positions with the Interior Design Educators Council, including past regional chair for the Midwest and associate editor of the *IDEC Exchange*. Harper is an active member of the American Society of Interior Designers. His research interests include the design of educational spaces, work styles and workplace strategy, and higher education pedagogy and practices. He has presented both nationally and internationally at many conferences.